A TREASURY OF

African-American

Christmas Stories

A TREASURY OF

African-American
Christmas Stories

Compiled and edited by

Bettye Collier-Thomas

ILLUSTRATED BY JAMES REYNOLDS

Henry Holt and Company
New York

Henry Holt and Company, Inc.
Publishers since 1866
115 West 18th Street
New York, New York 10011

Henry Holt® is a registered
trademark of Henry Holt and Company, Inc.

Library of Congress Cataloging-in-Publication Data
A treasury of African-American Christmas stories /
[compiled by] Bettye Collier-Thomas. —1st ed.
p.   cm.
ISBN 0-8050-5122-8 (alk. paper)
1. Christmas —Literary collections.   2. American literature —
Afro-American authors.   3. Afro-Americans —Literary collections.
I. Collier-Thomas, Bettye.
PS509.C56T73   1997   97-5459
810.8'0334 —dc21   CIP

Henry Holt books are available for special promotions
and premiums. For details contact: Director, Special Markets.

First Edition 1997

DESIGNED BY BETTY LEW
ILLUSTRATED BY JAMES REYNOLDS

Printed in the United States of America
All first editions are printed on acid-free paper. ∞

1   3   5   7   9   10   8   6   4   2

In Memory of My Grandparents

Luzella Veal Collier

and

William Thomas Collier

CONTENTS

Acknowledgments   *ix*
Note to Readers   *xi*
Introduction   *xiii*

❄

THE CHRISTMAS REUNION DOWN AT MARTINSVILLE
Augustus M. Hodges   *1*

❄

THE CHILDREN'S CHRISTMAS
Alice Moore Dunbar-Nelson   *13*

❄

CHRISTMAS EVE STORY
Fanny Jackson Coppin   *23*

❄

ELSIE'S CHRISTMAS
Salem Tutt Whitney   *33*

❄

BRO'R ABR'M JIMSON'S WEDDING: A CHRISTMAS STORY
Pauline E. Hopkins   *49*

❄

TWO CHRISTMAS DAYS: A HOLIDAY STORY
Ida Wells Barnett   *77*

❄

A CHRISTMAS PARTY THAT PREVENTED A SPLIT IN THE CHURCH
Margaret Black   *101*

❄

AFTER MANY DAYS: A CHRISTMAS STORY
Fannie Barrier Williams   *131*

❄

THE PRODIGAL DAUGHTER: A STORY OF THREE CHRISTMAS EVES
Augustus M. Hodges   *163*

❄

MIRAMA'S CHRISTMAS TEST
T. Thomas Fortune   *175*

❄

THREE MEN AND A WOMAN
Augustus M. Hodges   *187*

❄

Sources   *254*

ACKNOWLEDGMENTS

Charles J. Thomas, my husband, provided invaluable assistance in research that helped me to locate the ending of "Three Men and a Woman," and in the transcription of the Christmas stories. When my hands were strapped up and in pain from tendinitis, he volunteered to type the stories, and for this I am deeply indebted to him.

Gloria Harper Dickinson for years has encouraged me to empty some of my voluminous files and publish the long-forgotten works of many black writers and activists. It is because of her insistence that I decided to develop this collection of black Christmas stories.

Charlotte Sheedy and Neeti Madan, my literary agents, patiently listened to my discussion of these Christmas stories and encouraged me to prepare them for publication. They have waited four years for me to begin the process of publishing some of the many studies I have planned.

Tracy Sherrod, my editor, encouraged me to submit these stories and promised that it would be a beautiful book. And it is!

Farrah Jasmine Griffin and Catherine Thomas Matthews read the manuscript and made supportive comments. I would like to especially thank James Turner, V. P. Franklin, Alexis B. Henderson, and Barbara Younger Catchings for their very careful reading of all the stories, their keen editing insights, and the excellent suggestions they provided for improvement. I also wish to thank Willard B. Gatewood, Jr., for providing invaluable biographical information on Augustus M. Hodges.

x *Acknowledgments*

NOTE TO READERS

In these stories the original spelling, punctuation, paragraphing, and chapter and section divisions have been preserved, except in cases where there was inconsistency in spelling or obvious typographical errors. In a few instances, letters have been added to complete the spelling of a word or a word has been inserted to render a sentence more comprehensible. Several of the stories include dashes in place of the names of towns, cities, and institutions. Authors like Pauline E. Hopkins and Augustus M. Hodges are making the point that the story is true and that the name of the place or the specific institution is omitted to protect the identity of the participants. Although there are a few silent punctuation changes, most alterations are indicated with brackets.

Christmas is a very important time for celebration, reflection, and reunion in the black community. During slavery the holiday represented a time of temporary freedom, festivity, and feasting.

These eleven enchanting Christmas stories reveal the special significance of this holiday. They were first published in the late nineteenth and early twentieth centuries, dealing with many themes that are still relevant today. In "The Children's Christmas," "Christmas Eve Story," and "Elsie's Christmas," Alice Moore Dunbar-Nelson, Fanny Jackson Coppin, and Salem Tutt Whitney respectively emphasize the importance of this season for children and the need for society to address the poverty that plagued their lives. The central theme in Fannie Barrier Williams's "After Many Days" is the impact of slavery on black women. "Three Men and a Woman," written by Augustus M. Hodges, raises salient issues about race relations and miscegenation. "Elsie's Christmas," "Bro'r Abr'm Jimson's Wedding," "Two Christmas Days," "A Christmas Party That Prevented a Split in the Church," and "Mirama's

Christmas Test," written by Salem Tutt Whitney, Pauline E. Hopkins, Ida Wells Barnett, Margaret Black, and T. Thomas Fortune, respectively, share concerns about male-female relationships, emphasizing diverse themes. In "The Prodigal Daughter," Augustus M. Hodges relates the need for young black women to become involved in uplift work. As in all the stories, this one also reiterates the importance of family and community.

These works are a part of the African-American storytelling tradition that has taken literary form. The stories are grounded in the historical experiences of black people in this country. The Christmas theme is used somewhat as a pretext to explore larger issues in the African-American community, issues very closely related to the concerns and dilemmas black people faced from 1890 to 1915.

I'm sure you might be surprised that these well-known journalists, activists, national leaders, and spokespersons wrote fiction. It was their commitment to address the pressing issues confronting the African-American community and their high level of responsibility to positive race relations that encouraged them to use as many mediums as possible to get their messages across. Ida Wells Barnett was best known as a journalist and anti-lynching activist. Alice Moore Dunbar-Nelson and Fannie Barrier Williams are best remembered as social and political activists and Fanny Jackson Coppin was well known as an educator. T. Thomas Fortune established a formidable record as editor of the *New York Age,* while Salem Tutt Whitney distinguished himself as a stage performer and playwright. Yet all of these figures were writers, even though Pauline Elizabeth Hopkins, Augustus M. Hodges, and Margaret Black are the only people included who are identified primarily as novelists.

These literary gems were originally serialized in black-owned newspapers and periodicals, essential venues for the majority of black writers who were largely excluded from the white press. African-American publications provided these writers the freedom to address such issues as post-Reconstruction lynching, economic and social oppression, interracial relationships, and self-determination—topics white publishers, who were more interested in black caricature, deemed unacceptable. Black-owned publications, such as the *Indianapolis Freeman, Christian Recorder, Baltimore Afro-American,* and *Colored American,* were among the most influential African-American newspapers and journals in the country. These publications presented an opportunity for blacks to converse among themselves about their conditions and to develop their own social and political philosophy.

These Christmas stories are reflections of black thought and life during a tumultuous era. They indicate how varied, complex, and exciting the world in which they lived was, and how similar issues still concern us today.

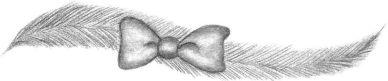

The Christmas Reunion Down at Martinsville

AUGUSTUS M. HODGES

Augustus M. Hodges

In "The Christmas Reunion Down at Martinsville," Augustus Michael Hodges presents an African-American version of a Christmas poem.

Hodges, a prominent New York writer well known to readers of the major black newspapers, magazines, and journals of his time, is, like many early black journalists and literary figures, waiting to be "discovered." I. Garland Penn, in *The Afro-American Press, and Its Editors* (1891), stated that "he has few superiors in the journalistic field." His extensive news columns appeared regularly in black newspapers under his pen name B. Square, and his poems, jokes, and short stories are widely represented in the leading black as well as white press of the time. He was elected to the Virginia House of Delegates in 1876, and during the late nineteenth and early twentieth centuries he wrote for a variety of black newspapers, including the *New York Globe* and the *Indianapolis Freeman,* where he began as a staff correspondent in 1889. In 1890, Hodges began publication of the *Brooklyn Sentinel,* which was published for three years. In the early 1890s, he was a candidate for the position of U.S. Minister to Haiti, receiving the endorsement of over five hundred leading Republicans.

Born in Williamsburg, Virginia, on March 18, 1854, Augustus attended and, in 1874, graduated from the Hampton Normal and Industrial Institute. He was the son of Willis Hodges, a pioneering African-American journalist and well-known abolitionist and personal friend of the notorious John Brown. After the Civil War, Willis Hodges was elected to the Virginia State Senate, and served as a U.S. Elector from Princess Anne County, Virginia. In an article discussing "Passing for White," Augustus Hodges intimated that his great-grandmother on his father's side was a young white Englishwoman; however, he noted that his appearance belied that fact. Following his father's death, Augustus published Willis's autobiography in the *Indianapolis Freeman*. In 1982, in *Free Man of Color,* Willard B. Gatewood, Jr., resurrected Willis Hodges.

In 1894, Hodges and several other black literary figures formed a stock company known as the Augustus M. Hodges Literary Syndicate to publish black novels and short stories in what he described as "cheap paper-cover book form." From 1894 to around 1905, the *Indianapolis Freeman* purchased many of his stories from this organization.

Hodges's stories reflect the full spectrum of black life and culture and incorporate his belief that "an author must use the words of others in his song or story, and more especially if the said song or story is a true one." Thus, his poems and stories, such as "The Christmas Reunion Down at Martinsville" (1894), "Three Men and a Woman" (1902–1903), and "The Prodigal Daughter" (1904), mirror the beliefs, values, speech, habits, and traditions of African Americans. Hodges prided himself on the realism reflected in his writings. In 1897, in a preface to "'Twas Not to Be! Or Cupid's Battle for Miscegenation," he stated that one of the motives that prompted him to write was fame, and that if he reached his goal through writing, it would be "by facts, not fiction; by truth, not imagination." Moreover, repeating Hodges's claim, one newspaper editor stated that "All of his novels [sic] are founded upon facts. The leading characters are real and their doings real. Their names and locations have, however, been changed; their doings painted with fiction and the links of the events connected with the romantic imagination of the author, guided by twenty-odd years of careful study of the doings of both races."

"The Christmas Reunion Down at Martinsville" is set in Martinsville, Kentucky, around 1893. As three generations of a family gather to celebrate Christmas, Uncle Joe Moore, the narrator and patriarch, reminisces about how he and Aunt Sallie met some forty years earlier in Kentucky. Through the use of narrative, Augustus Hodges manages a number of important themes—the horrors of slavery, the treatment of women, the love between black men and women, the meaning of freedom, the strength of familial bonds, African-American embracement of the Protestant work ethic, and the bravery of black men.

Hodges presents the characters Uncle Joe and Aunt Sallie as bound by the restrictions of slavery, particularly as it affected patterns of courtship and marriage. He demonstrates the types of risks slave men and women took to be together.

Hodges also develops certain white characters, representatives primarily of the slaveholding class. The portrayal of Tom Scott, a patroller, suggests the surveillance and control exerted to police the movement of slaves so as to prevent their running away, the licentiousness of white men who showed no respect for the virtue of black women, and the problems black men encountered when they attempted to defend themselves or their women. Defending Sallie's honor, Uncle Joe fought Tom Scott and his brother Ed and won. Although his life was spared, his owner sold him to a slave trader the next day. After two and a half months on a farm in eastern Tennessee, he ran away with a fellow slave. They succeeded in reaching Kentucky, where he married Sallie.

Hodges's white characters run the gamut from patrollers, slave trader, and preacher to President of the United States. The first two are the embodiment of evil; the latter two are redeemed by their humanitarian acts. For a small price the preacher willingly married slaves, and President Abraham Lincoln issued the Emancipation Proclamation which presaged the freeing of the slaves.

Hodges also demonstrates the bravery of slaves who joined the Union Army and fought in the Civil War. Utilizing Uncle Joe as narrator and having him reflect upon his and Sallie's lives as slaves and free persons enables Hodges to demonstrate the strong bond of love that some black men and women were able to develop. In describing the Christmas celebration as a reunion, he emphasizes the importance of family and tradition. And finally as Uncle Joe describes how the children worked hard to buy the land and build a house for their parents and how they succeeded in making a living, Hodges demonstrates that African Americans embraced the Protestant work ethic and worked together to ensure the success of their families.

The Christmas Reunion Down at Martinsville

'Twas a bright Christmas morning in M —— "Old Kentucky,"
Aunt Sallie was busy disrobing a duck;
A featherless turkey close by her side lay,
Prepared for the dinner that bright Christmas day.
'Twas a family reunion, and Uncle Joe Moore
And his good wife, Aunt Sallie, both ten and three score,
Had gathered around them, their "girls" and their "boys,"
With their children's children—the grand parents' toys.
The "girls" (all past thirty) were helping to make
The "sweet tater puddin's," the pies and the cake.
The "boys" and the grand boys, the fires were making,
The oldest grand daughter the biscuits were baking;
The little grand children, a dozen or more,
Were having a good time just outside the door;
While Uncle Joe Moore, the venerable sire,
Sat smoking his pipe, with his feet by the fire.

When the clock tolled the mid day, the feast was complete,
And after each member had taken his seat,
The venerable sire stood up by his chair,
And with arms up-lifted he offered this prayer:
"We thank Thee, our Father in heaven," he said,
"For the abundance of good things before us now spread;
We thank Thee dear Lord, that me and my wife
Have been spared, by thy goodness, to reach an old life;
We thank Thee, of all things, the most and the best,
To meet all our children, from North, South and West.
Continue Thy blessings, Thy goodness and love,
And prepare us to meet Thee, in heaven above."
The grace being over, the feast was begun,
The duck and the turkey were carved one by one;
The big chicken pot-pie received the same fate,
A super-abundance was piled on each plate.
After the meats came the puddings and pies,
Then how the grand children all opened their eyes
When one of their uncles from up Illinois,
Brought out from the closet a basket of toys.
As dinner was over, the venerable sire,
Got up from his seat and stood by the fire.
He called to his side each lamb of his fold,

     Augustus M. Hodges

And blessed and caressed them, as Jacob of old.
"What changes we've seen Sal," remarked Uncle Joe,
"These years we've been married, some forty or so;
'Twas, let me see, forty? Yes, forty-one years
Since the Christmas we first met at Uncle Bill Stears.
I remember, ole 'oman, you looked mighty gran',
And I was then, children, a good lookin' man.
I walked with your mother from Clayton that night,
And 'fore we got home, why, I got in a fight;
Tom Scott, a patroller, insulted your mother,
And I knocked him down, and Ed., his big brother.
I then asked your mother if she'd be my wife.
Her answer was, 'Yes Joe, since you risked your life
For me up the road, and licked ole Tom Scott —
Why, I'll be your wife, why Joseph why not?'
But the next day, my children, my master sold me
To an ole 'nigger trader' from East Tennessee.
There I worked on a farm without seeing your mother
For eighty long days, 'till me and another
Plantation hand run away, and met with good luck,
For we soon found ourself on the shores of Kentuck
Before my ole white folks knowed I run er way.
We two was married that same Christmas day.

We was married at Scottsville by ole Pete Brown,
He was a white preacher, who lived in the town,
And would marry we slave folks, no matter or not,
If our masters was willing, if he only got
A two dollar bill, or a big barrel of corn.
And the very next Christmas our Lucy was born.
The next of the past that I now can remember,
Was when we moved here, Sal, the following September;
And then came the war, Sal, and old master died,
While Missus and you, Sal, stood by his side.
Then I left you and the children, and went out to fight
For the Union and freedom, one warm summer's night.
Then good Abraham Lincoln he sot us all free,
And we had in Martinsville, a big jubilee;
Then you boys and you girls all worked hand to hand,
To buy me and your mother this house and this land.
Then some of you married, and some went out West,
While me and your mother, along with the rest,
Stayed on the old homestead and worked night and day,
A farming and trucking, and made the work pay.
We are glad for to meet you all back here once more,
And see all your dear babies together, before
Me and your mother, for we're both old and gray,

  Augustus M. Hodges

Receive old death's summons to call us away.
God bless you and keep you through life, is my prayer."
And the venerable sire sat down in his chair.
The rest of the evening was spent in a measure,
Receiving old friends, or by chatting in pleasure
Till long after midnight, with hearts light and gay —
'Twas a happy reunion, a bright Christmas day.

The Children's Christmas

ALICE MOORE DUNBAR-NELSON

Alice Moore Dunbar-Nelson

Educator, author, and social and political activist, Alice Moore Dunbar-Nelson received her first recognition as the wife of celebrated poet and novelist Paul Laurence Dunbar and was later acclaimed as a Harlem Renaissance poet. Born in New Orleans, Louisiana, on July 19, 1875, Alice Ruth Moore was one of two daughters of Joseph Moore, a Creole seaman, and Patricia Wright Moore. She attended elementary and high school in New Orleans and graduated from the two-year teacher training program at Straight College (now Dillard University). She later studied at Cornell and Columbia universities and the University of Pennsylvania, where she specialized in psychology and English educational testing. Beginning her teaching career in New Orleans in 1892, except for brief interruptions, she taught school for almost four decades.

In 1895, Alice Moore completed her first book, *Violets and Other Tales,* and began a romance with Paul Laurence Dunbar, who gained great fame for his Negro dialect verse. In 1897, she moved from

Boston to New York City, where she accepted a public school teaching position in Brooklyn and assisted Victoria Earle Matthews in establishing in Harlem the White Rose Mission, a home for girls. It was in December 1897 that she wrote "The Children's Christmas," a story which reflected the lives of the children whom she taught.

"The Children's Christmas" is the story of five children, from different racial and ethnic backgrounds, who live in a large city. These children represent all children, through circumstances not of their making, who do not experience the joy, the spirit, and the meaning of Christmas. This social commentary by Moore is presented as a panorama to show how many children at the turn of the century did not celebrate the "luxury" of a real Christmas.

Julia is an unkempt seven-year-old who attends school mostly in the afternoons to reduce the necessity for breakfast. She lives with her mother, who drinks excessively and physically abuses her. When asked, "What will Santa bring you?" she replied, "Nothin' but another beatin'." Although Moore does not identify the child as being African American, the use of dialect suggests that she was.

Matilda is a Jewish girl who attends the same school as Julia. She lives in an orphanage. Being Jewish, she does not understand or celebrate Christmas, but she accepts Santa Claus and the traditional role he plays. Santa brings toys and Matilda would love to get a doll for Christmas.

Florence is too young for school, so she gets to play outdoors during the day. She views Christmas as a cold, uncomfortable time of the year. Poorly dressed in hand-me-down clothes, toys would not be number one on her list to Santa.

Frank, who is the nursemaid to his baby brother, wanders with his charge through the streets taking in all the beautiful decorations and hoopla of the holiday season. He gazes in the store windows knowing that his wish for even one toy would be in vain. Santa Claus would not stop by his house.

Hattie, almost blind since the age of six, cannot see the beautifully decorated store windows and other adornments of Christmas. But she can hear the joyful talk and sounds of the season. Is her wish for Christmas the gift of seeing?

Moore reminds the readers that Christmas is the children's time, and regardless of race, gender, religion, or circumstance, all children should be given the opportunity to participate in this joyous occasion. She reminds the more fortunate in society that they should live up to the true spirit of Christmas and share their good fortune with those who are less fortunate.

It is most likely that the setting for this story is Brooklyn, New York, in 1897, the year that Alice Ruth Moore taught in a public school there. Moore, who was only twenty-two at the time this story was written, was struck with the plight of these children. Her concluding statement that "these little folks are not imaginary small personages created for Sunday-school literature and sentimental dissertations on so-called sociology. They are actual, evident, their counterparts around us, no matter where we may live" suggests that she wrote the story to illustrate the plight of many urban children who lived in poverty and despair. As a budding young crusader, she embodied the spirit of the Progressive Era (1890–1920) and believed that one should use all resources to bring public attention to the conditions that existed in society.

The Children's Christmas

With the tinkle of joy-bells in the air, the redolence of pine and the untasted anticipation of saccharine joys to be, the child steps forward into the full heyday of his prerogatives. For this is childhood's time—it is the commemoration of a child's birth and the gifts brought him. It is a time of peace and gladness, say the children; it is our reign of love and gift-giving.

Yet, even the small kings and queens who reign over this carnival of joy are not happy. There are many who have never come into their kingdom at all—to whom the luxury of a real Christmas would be a foretaste of Paradise. Did you ever stop to think of this? You who are pushing and jostling in the shopping crowd, your arms full of expensive toys, your heart full of cheery cares lest some one be forgotten? We might have a little panorama for your especial benefit if you do not mind.

Julia is in school. She is seven and as unkempt as the school authorities will permit her. She is frequently absent from the morning session. We wondered why until we learned that her mother was "mos' all the time drunk" and didn't get up mornings, so Julia slept too to reduce the necessity for breakfast, and came straggling in, in the afternoon, half stupid, wholly indifferent.

"What will Santa bring you," asked her nearest neighbor in school during a lively discussion about Christmas.

She shrugged her tiny shoulders, "Nothin' but another beatin' I guess." And the nearest neighbor turned away to tell her chosen friend that as she had four dolls now she didn't want another one just yet.

Matilda is in the same school. She is a swarthy, pretty black-eyed Hebrew. Her black locks are cropped short. She wears the uniform of an asylum not far away. Christmas? It is incomprehensible to her. Who was the Christ child? Why keep his birthday? But Santa Klaus she understands, and the gifts that are denied her. Dolls! why to possess even the tiniest one would seem too much happiness for a mortal Hebrew maiden. As she heard the other children enumerating their toys it seemed to her wonderful that they did not unfurl wings, for surely angels are so blessed. Why if she only had the wee smallest toy she would never need to speak in school again, so complete would be the measure of her bliss.

Florence is on the other side of the river and too small to be in school. So when it is warm she plays in the sunshine which freely attempts to clear the stagnant atmosphere. When the winds nip through from river to river she seeks shelter in a tenement, dark and fetid and noisy with brawls and drunkenness. Christmas? It means cold weather and shivering in a poor, thin jacket whose warmth was a thing of the past when it fell to her two years ago. Toys? Once she actually touched the dress of a gorgeously dressed lady doll, and the memory of it was like wine for weeks. Even now she regarded that hand in some measure as sacred.

Frank stands musingly before a window resplendent with gold and silver Christmas tree "fixin's." The poor child gazing hungrily in brilliant windows at holiday time is a figure that is well-nigh threadbare in juvenile fiction, but it is so pitifully, painfully true and ever-recurring. He clutches his baby brother by the arm and dreamfully wonders if there was ever one person on earth who was rich enough to buy all that. Baby brother grows impatient, for he is whimsical, and nurse Frank moves away sighing hopelessly. It was like longing for ice cream the year round to even dare wish for one toy.

Hattie listens to the Christmas talk and the Christmas noise and the fakir's wondrous stream of unchecked gab, and wrinkles her little face painfully. You see she is almost blind, and objects are but an indistinct blur to her. Blind at six through carelessness and ignorance, with not a helping hand that will lead her to a dispensary for treatment. She cannot see the wondrous windows; she can only hear and wonder. Who knows if in her gropings, mental as well as physical, there does not form the faultily famed wish for the Christmas present of seeing?

  Alice Moore Dunbar-Nelson

These little folks are not imaginary small personages created for Sunday-school literature and sentimental dissertations on so-called sociology. They are actual, evident, their counterparts around us, no matter where we may live. They have been robbed of the most precious birthright that Heaven bestows—their childhood, and their annual birth-feast is denied them—not because the world wishes them ill, but because the world is scarcely cognizant of their existence. And yet "Christmas is the children's time, the day of their rejoicing." Does it seem fair that to the least of them there does not filter some minute molecule of the general happiness, some infinitesimal spangled toy that would never be missed from the more fortunate ones?

Christmas Eve Story

F A N N Y   J A C K S O N   C O P P I N

Fanny Jackson Coppin

A well-known educator, civic and religious activist, and feminist, Fanny Muriel Jackson was born a slave in Washington, D.C. Her freedom was purchased by Sarah Clark, her aunt. At a relatively young age, she was sent to live with another aunt in New Bedford, Massachusetts, where she worked as a domestic. At the age of fourteen she went to live with a relative in Newport, Rhode Island, where she worked for six years as a servant in the home of George Henry Calvert, a writer and the great-grandson of Lord Baltimore, who settled Maryland. It was during those years that she attended public school and became determined to "get an education and become a teacher of my people."

Fanny Jackson passed the entrance examination for the Rhode Island State Normal School at Bristol. Following completion of the course of study there, she decided to attend Oberlin College in Ohio in 1860, one of the few white colleges in America which admitted African Americans. At Oberlin she pursued the classical course, known as the gentleman's course of study. The faculty did not prevent women from taking the classical course, but they did not advise it. As the course emphasized Latin, Greek, and mathematics, it was felt that women would not fare well. After a year in the literary course, Fanny entered the regular classical course.

Fanny graduated from Oberlin in 1865 and accepted an appointment to teach at the Institute for Colored Youth, a school established in Philadelphia in 1837 by the Quakers. During the antebellum period, this school developed quite a reputation for its excellent teachers and classical curriculum and for the quality of its graduates. The Institute was a showplace which was visited by interested persons from different parts of the United States and Europe. Contrary to the belief of many whites that blacks were inferior and suited only for menial labor, the Institute was evidence that blacks could acquire a higher level of education. Fanny taught Greek, Latin, and mathematics and served as principal of the girls' high school department. She was delighted to teach black children and to see them master Caesar, Virgil, Cicero, Horace, and Xenophon's *Anabasis*.

In 1869, the general principal of the Institute, Ebenezer D. Bassett, was appointed U.S. Minister to Haiti by President Ulysses S. Grant. Fanny Jackson replaced him as head principal, becoming the first black woman to hold a position at that level in an educational institution. During her tenure of thirty-seven years at the Institute, a number of important black leaders came under her tutelage, and she was influential in the shaping of some of the major patterns of black education in the late nineteenth century.

In 1881, Fanny married the Reverend Levi Jenkins Coppin, a noted minister and bishop of the African Methodist Episcopal Church (A.M.E.). Although she had been in the Baptist Church, Mrs. Coppin became involved in the A.M.E. Church. She was active in the missionary field and as president of the Women's Home and Foreign Missionary Society. In 1888, she was a delegate to the Centenary Conference on the Protestant Missions of the World, held in London. At that meeting she spoke forcefully about the intelligence of African-American women and the tremendous responsibilities they assumed in every field of endeavor, including missions. In 1893, she delivered the same message at the Chicago World's Fair.

Although she is best remembered for her work in education, Fanny Jackson Coppin was also widely known as a writer, lecturer, and organizer in the black woman's club movement. "Christmas Eve Story," published under her maiden name, reflects her concerns for poor black children, and illustrates the plight of many that she came in daily contact with in the alleys and hovels where they lived in Philadelphia. This short story is written in the style of a fairy tale with an appeal to very young readers and listeners. It opens on Christmas Eve, 1879, and concludes on Christmas Eve, 1880. The reference to

Acorn Alley and the almshouse suggests a large city, most likely Philadelphia, where Fanny Jackson resided.

In December 1880, "Christmas Eve Story" was published in the *Christian Recorder,* the organ of the African Methodist Episcopal Church, which was one of the earliest black publications to publish the literary efforts of African Americans. Its diverse offerings attracted wide readership among black Methodists and appealed to a broad-based national African-American audience. The story makes an appeal for the community to address the poverty experienced by so many black children who lived in filthy alleys infested with disease.

Christmas Eve Story

Once upon a time, there was a little girl named Maggie Devins, and she had a brother named Johnny, just one year older than she. Here they both are. Now if they could they would get up and make you a bow. But dear me! we all get so fastened down in pictures that we have to keep as quiet as mice, or we'd tear the paper all to pieces. I'm going to tell you something about this little boy and girl, and perhaps some little reader will remember it. You see how very clean and neat both of them look. Well, if you had seen them when Grandma Devins first found them you never would have thought that they could be made to look as nice as this. Now hear their story:

Last Christmas Eve while Grandma Devins was sitting by her bright fire, there was a loud knock at the door, and upon opening it, she found a policeman who had in his arms two children who were nearly dead.

"I come, mum," he said, "to ask you, if you will let these poor little young ones stay here to-night in your kitchen; their mother has just died from the fever. She lived in an old hovel around in Acorn Alley, and I'm afraid to leave the young ones there to-night, for they're half starved and half frozen to death now. God pity the poor, mum, God pity the poor, for it's hard upon them, such weather as this."

Meanwhile, Grandma Devins had pulled her big sofa up to the fire and was standing looking down upon the dirty and pinched little faces before her. She didn't say anything, but she just kept looking at the children and wiping her eyes and blowing her nose. All at once she turned around as if she had been shot; she flew to the pantry and brought out some milk which she put on the fire to boil. And very soon she had two steaming cups of hot milk with nice biscuit broken into it, and with this she fed the poor little creatures until a little color came into their faces, and she knew that she had given them enough for that time.

The policeman said he would call for the children in the morning and take them to the almshouse. The fact is the policeman was a kind-hearted man, and he secretly hoped that he could get some one to take the children and be kind to them.

As soon as Maggie and Johnny had their nice warm milk they began to talk. Johnny asked Grandma Devins if she had anybody to give her Christmas presents, and Grandma said, "no." But Maggie spoke up and said her mamma told her before she died that God always gave Christmas presents to those who had no one to give them any. And throwing her arms around Grandma's neck she said, "God will not forget you, dear lady, for you've been so good to us." Like a flash of light it passed through Grandma Devins' mind that God had sent her these children as her Christmas gift. So she said at once:

"Children, I made a mistake. I *have* had a Christmas present."

"There," said Maggie, "I knew you would get one; I knew it." When the policeman came in the morning his heart was overjoyed to see the "young ones," as he called them, nicely washed and sitting by the fire bundled up in some of Grandma Devins' dresses. She had burnt every stitch of the dirty rags which they had on the night before. So that accounted for their being muffled up so.

"You can go right away, policeman; these children are my Christmas gift, and please God I'll be mother and father both, to the poor little orphans."

A year has passed since then, and she says that Johnny and Maggie are the best Christmas gifts that any old woman ever had. She has taught Maggie to darn and sew neatly, and one of these days she will be able to earn money as a seamstress. Have you noticed her little needle-case hanging against the wall? Do you see the basket of apples on one side? Johnny was paring them when Maggie asked him to show her about her arithmetic, for Johnny goes to school, but Maggie stays at home and helps Grandma. Now as soon as Grandma comes back she is going to make them some mince pies for Christmas. Johnny will finish paring the apples, while Maggie is stoning the raisins. Oh! what a happy time they will have to-morrow. For I will whisper in your ear, little reader, that Grandma Devins is going to bring home something else with her other than raisins. The same kind-hearted policeman who I told you about in the beginning, has made Johnny a beautiful sled, and painted the name "Hero" on it. Grandma has bought for Maggie the nicest little hood and cloak that ever you saw. Is that not nice? I guess if they knew what they're going to get they wouldn't sit so quietly as we see them; they'd jump up and dance about the floor, even if they tore the paper all to pieces. Oh! let every little girl thank our heavenly father for the blessed gift of His dear Son on the first Christmas Day, eighteen hundred and eighty years ago.

Elsie's Christmas

SALEM TUTT WHITNEY

Salem Tutt Whitney

Salem Tutt Whitney was born in Logansport, Indiana, in 1869. The oldest child of a struggling itinerant minister, at an early age he quit school for a short period of time to work. Eventually he graduated from Shortridge High School in Indianapolis and then attended DePauw University where he studied for the ministry. Except for brief employment as the minister of a church in Titusville, Pennsylvania, he enjoyed a distinguished career as a stage performer, playwright, producer, comedian, poet, and journalist. His first stage performance was in 1895, singing bass with the Puggsley Brothers' Tennessee Warblers, a minstrel company.

In 1899, Whitney formed a company, the Oriental Troubadours, an aggregation of twenty-eight people and a nine-piece band. He toured the country with this group for seven years. In 1901, he opened his first musical comedy, *The Ex-President of Liberia*. Whitney wrote the book and music, staged the entire show, arranged the numbers, and designed the costumes. His brother, J. Homer Tutt, was his understudy for this production. The two of them later made the names Tutt and Whitney famous. In 1906, he joined the S. H. Dudley Smart Set Company, and in 1907, Homer and Salem went with Black Patti's Troubadours as Whitney and Tutt, the beginning of the famous combination. A couple of years later, in 1909, they organized the second company of the original Smart Set Company, and in 1916 they gained control of the company and renamed it Whitney and Tutt's Smarter Set Company.

Between 1909 and 1922, Whitney wrote a big two-act musical comedy for every theatrical season. From 1910 to 1914, the Smart Set was one of only four major black road companies in the field. Whitney and Tutt were a key link in the black show business world between the famous Williams and Walker team and Black Patti to Irvin Miller and Billy King.

As a journalist, Whitney wrote a theatrical column for a number of newspapers, including the *Chicago Defender*.

In "Elsie's Christmas," published by the *Indianapolis Freeman* in 1912, Salem Tutt Whitney tells the traditional story of Christmas and the role of Santa Claus. He touches upon a number of issues which confronted African-American families by showing that the love between black men and women can be strained by economic and political forces outside of their control. He also emphasizes the problems single women have when they must support their children on their own. Thus he argues for black men and women to be more sensitive and understanding of each others' needs.

"Elsie's Christmas" could be set at any time and in any place. However, Elsie's request for a doll with "the pretty brown face and Indian hair" suggests that the story occurs at some point between 1908 and 1912. Although so-called Negro dolls were available during the 1890s, most were produced by white factories and had what some considered "uncomely and deformed features." In 1908, the National Baptist Convention set the pace for production of "Negro Doll Babies for Negro Children." The movement for black dolls was one indication of the growing African-American race consciousness so evident during the first and second decades of the twentieth century, which became full-blown in the New Negro Movement of the 1920s. Although dolls with brown faces appeared, they all had straight hair, or what Elsie called "Indian hair."

In addition to reinforcing the theme of racial pride, Whitney in referring to the two female characters, Vergie and Elsie, as Mrs. Waterman and "little Lady" subtly introduces the issue of respect for black womanhood. White Americans frequently addressed black men and women by their first names, or called them girls, boys, aunties, and uncles. To negate this pattern of disrespect, blacks would not use their first names but would refer to themselves only as Mr. or Mrs. with their surname.

"Little Lady" was given to Elsie as a pet name by her mother, "Mrs. Waterman." As Whitney explains in the story, Mrs. Waterman "had also explained to her [Elsie] the full significance of the word 'lady,' and how important it was for her daughter to have all the requisites of a lady." This statement and the use of the term suggests that black women were concerned about the image of black womanhood, an issue used by Ida Wells Barnett and the National Association of Colored Women to thwart the proliferation of negative images of African-American women, who were frequently depicted by white leaders and the white press as being women of loose morals. Mrs. Waterman stressed to Elsie that if one is to be considered a lady she must conduct herself in that manner, meaning she must be refined and have "gentle manners" and must receive the "homage or devotion" of her husband or lover.

Finally, in the best of African-American traditions, the story speaks of the power of prayer. Elsie was taught that if she "prayed to the Good Man for anything I really wanted or needed, and believed that He would give me what I asked for, He'd do it." In the depths of slavery when there seemingly was no hope, black slaves also believed that God would answer their prayers. God answered Elsie's and Mrs. Waterman's prayers because they had been good and had faith.

Elsie's Christmas

❦

"Mamma, how old is Santa Claus?"

Mrs. Waterman was making a melancholy inspection of her clean but meagerly furnished kitchen. She turned at the sound of Elsie's voice and looked at her youthful questioner. She noted the perfect oval of the little girl's face, the healthy color, the beautiful coal-black eyes and the dark brown hair curling rebelliously away from the intelligent forehead. As Mrs. Waterman made this rapid inventory of Elsie's charms, her face became suffused with a smile of motherly pride, in which love, tenderness, and solicitude were equally blended.

In the year that they had been alone, Mrs. Waterman had never grown used to Elsie's puzzling and startling questions. Elsie's mind seemed unusually mature for a girl six years of age. No matter how trivial the questions, Mrs. Waterman always considered them seriously, knowing that intelligent answers would help develop her daughter's intellect. So now, as she looked at Elsie's expectant face, she pondered her answer.

"Santa Claus is very old," she answered gravely; "very, very old, little Lady."

"Little Lady" was the pet name Mrs. Waterman had given her daughter. She had also explained to her the full significance of the word "lady," and how important it was for her daughter to have all the requisites of a lady. Elsie was very proud of the name.

"Is he as old as papa?" asked Elsie, after a childish attempt to compute the years necessary to make one very, very old.

At the word "papa" a pained expression came into Mrs. Waterman's face, but it was only momentary and passed unnoticed by Elsie.

"Very much older than your—papa," Mrs. Waterman answered, thoughtfully.

"I guess he must be older than grandpop, too," mused Elsie; "his hair looks whiter and his beard longer in the pictures I see of him. Did anybody ever see Santa Claus when he was little?"

"Yes," answered the mother.

"Who?" eagerly questioned Elsie.

"It is a story, little Lady," replied Mrs. Waterman.

"Oh! little mother, tell it to me, won't you, please?" pleaded Elsie.

Mrs. Waterman, glad of the opportunity to rest, seated herself in a chair near the window. Elsie climbed eagerly upon her knee, threw her chubby arms affectionately about her mother's neck and kissed her full upon the lips. With all the infinite love of a mother showing in her face, made radiant by the holiest of passions, Mrs. Waterman pressed the child to her bosom.

The winter's sun, like a golden globe of unquenchable fire, was sinking slowly below the horizon; its yellow rays smiled through the window and formed a halo around the little girl's head. A flood of tenderness swelled in the mother's bosom, bringing tears to her eyes, and she knew how the Virgin Mary must have felt when first she gazed upon her infant Jesus.

"Why do we celebrate Christmas?" asked Mrs. Waterman.

"Because Christ our Savior was born upon that day," promptly responded Elsie.

"More than two thousand years ago," began Mrs. Waterman, "Melchior, Gaspar, and Balthazar, three very wise men, had heard that Jesus was to be born in Bethlehem of Judea. Melchior was a Greek, Gaspar was a Hindoo, and Balthazar was an Egyptian. They lived very far apart, but each was told in a dream that he should see the Savior. Their hearts were filled with joy and thanksgiving, for they had never thought to have the privilege of gazing upon their Savior in person. The Spirit of God guided each one to a common meeting place: from there they were told to follow a star which was set in the heavens to guide them.

"Without doubt or misgiving they followed the star until it stopped over a stable in the little town of Bethlehem. 'This must be the place;

we will enter,' said they. Trembling with hope and fear they entered, and there they saw the baby Jesus, sleeping in its mother's arms.

"The wise men knelt down and worshiped Jesus. Then they laid at his feet costly presents of frankincense, myrrh, incense, gold and precious jewels. It was then that Santa Claus was born. Santa Claus is the Spirit of Thankfulness that finds expression in gifts, and it will live so long as Christ shall reign upon earth and fill the hearts of men and women with His goodness and love."

"Does he always come to good little girls and good little boys?" asked Elsie, after she had thought awhile over the story.

"Always," answered Mrs. Waterman, slowly.

"Haven't I been a good little girl, little mother?" said Elsie wistfully.

"No little girl could have been better, my Lady," replied the mother, and again a pained expression crept into her face.

"I hope Santa will bring me the doll with the pretty brown face and Indian hair, that I asked him for in my letter." Then a happy look came to Elsie's eyes. "Do you remember, little mother, you said if I prayed to the Good Man for anything I really wanted or needed, and believed that He would give me what I asked for, He'd do it?"

"I remember, little Lady," answered Mrs. Waterman.

"Well," continued Elsie. "I want my papa very, very much, and I want a dolly, but mostly I want my papa, and I'm going to ask the Good

Man to tell Santa to bring them to me tonight, so they will be here tomorrow for Christmas."

After stating her resolution, Elsie slipped down from her mother's knee and prepared for bed, filled with the happy anticipation that floods the hearts of children the world over on Christmas eve.

For more than an hour Mrs. Waterman sat by the bedside of the slumbering child. It was the bitterest hour of her life. "If it wasn't for the little Lady, I wouldn't mind," she sobbed; "if it wasn't for little Lady, I wouldn't mind." Then she thought of the first happy months after she had married Fred. How happy and full of manly pride he had been when she confided the secret that she was soon to be a mother. She remembered how tenderly solicitous he was during the trying period that preceded Elsie's birth. Then the baby had come, and Fred seemed to have eyes and ears for nothing but the baby. Jealousy, like a serpent, had crept into her heart. She felt that she hated the baby and her husband also. Her mild manners and sweet disposition underwent a complete change. She became crabbed and cranky. Fred, at a loss to account for the sudden change in his wife, bore her continued ill-temper with patience and fortitude; but he continually lavished the affection of his generous heart more and more upon his daughter. The years dragged slowly by; but the strain they were undergoing told on each, until the year before it had reached the breaking point.

Mrs. Waterman remembered vividly that last Christmas. Fred had promised her a set of white furs. Just before Christmas he told her that

  Salem Tutt Whitney

his work had slackened and that she must wait until the New Year for her furs; in the meantime he had spent all his savings for Elsie's Christmas. How mean and selfish she had thought him then! They quarreled, and she had told him to go; angry at her injustice, he had taken her at her word and left.

For weeks after her father had gone, Elsie had refused to be comforted. Mrs. Waterman was forced to tell Elsie the one and only falsehood she had ever told her, that her father was away on business and would be back as soon as possible. It was during the following weeks and months of loneliness that Mrs. Waterman had learned to love her daughter. She saw herself as she had been, a narrow-minded, selfish woman. "If Fred would only return," she murmured, "how different I would be!"

Mrs. Waterman had been put to her wits' end to provide for the little household. Not having been schooled in the art of economizing, her expenses were always more than her income. She had been forced to the humiliating expedient of pawning her jewelry; then her clothes, and lastly the furniture. Now it was Christmas eve, and not a cent to buy Elsie a present. How could she face the disappointed look of Elsie's bright eyes when they opened in the morning and found that Santa had passed her by? As the thought took full possession of Mrs. Waterman's mind, she fell upon her knees and sobbed in anguish. Then she prayed, "O God, send my husband to me! Give my baby her Christmas!"

A loud knock at the door brought Mrs. Waterman to her feet in quick alarm. She pressed her hand to her heart to still its tumultuous beating. The knock was repeated, this time louder, as if the knocker were growing impatient. Not knowing what to expect, she opened the door, and gazed in the face of a special delivery boy.

"Is this 332 X. street?" the boy asked.

"It is," Mrs. Waterman replied.

"A package for you." And the boy shoved a large box into her hands.

"There must be some mistake," began Mrs. Waterman, but the boy was walking rapidly away, whistling with pleasure that his last errand had been completed.

Trembling with excitement, Mrs. Waterman proceeded to undo the package. The first thing that greeted her eyes was a beautiful brown-skin doll. "Oh, how happy Lady will be!" she exclaimed. Smiling through her tears at the thought of Elsie's happiness, she proceeded to remove a layer of tissue paper, and there disclosed to her view was a set of handsome snow-white furs. Laughing and crying by turns, she fell upon her knees and buried her face in its soft fleece. "Fred has not forgotten us, little Lady," she whispered.

While Mrs. Waterman was yet upon her knees, the familiar melody of a whistler was borne to her ears. Only one person had ever whistled that little melody; could it be him, she wondered? Fred had always repeated the little strain at the next corner, so she would always be sure it was him. Now she waited breathlessly for the repetition; her nerves were strained to their utmost tension. Then, just as she was sure it would not recur, clear and sweet, the little melody broke upon the midnight air. Every doubt was dispelled. It was Fred! She arose from her knees. Her trembling knees threatened to give way and leave her sprawled upon the floor; she grasped the foot of the bed for support; the blood had receded from her face, leaving it pale and cold.

Now she could hear his footfalls upon the gravel walk. She had always loved to hear his firm and regular tread. As the footfalls drew nearer the door, they hesitated, as if the walker were in doubt whether to proceed or retire. Mrs. Waterman felt that she would faint. The steps drew nearer; now they were crossing the little porch; they hesitated at the door a moment; then came a knock. Even in this Mrs. Waterman recognized her husband's thoughtfulness; he was afraid to enter without knocking, as was his custom, not knowing what effect his sudden appearance might have upon his family. Mrs. Waterman heard the knock and tried to answer; only an inarticulate sound issued from her dry and parched throat. Impatient at not receiving an answer to his knock and fearful that something might be wrong, Fred opened the door, stepped across the threshold and stood face to face with his wife.

They seemed incapable of speech. Mrs. Waterman swayed slightly, but recovered herself with an effort. The husband was the first to speak.

"Virgie," he said, and his voice sounded strange and unnatural; "Virgie," he repeated, "I couldn't stay away another minute; 'deed I couldn't."

Mrs. Waterman wondered if she would ever regain her power of speech.

"It didn't seem right," continued Fred, "to be away from you and Lady on Christmas day."

Mrs. Waterman stood like a graven image, with eyes riveted upon her husband's face.

"I—I—thought—you might—you might be a little glad to see me," faltered the man. There was a sound of tears in his voice as he continued: "If—if—you'll just let me spend Christmas with you—and Lady—I'll promise to go away and—and—never see you again."

This momentary weakness in the man touched the woman as nothing else could have done. All the love of a good and true woman shone in her eyes and suffused her face. With quivering lips she cried: "O Fred! Fred! how could you!" She took one step toward her husband, faltered, swayed; at one stride the husband had her in his arms, crushed to his breast; her arms were about his neck. "I've wanted you so much, Freddie boy, so very, very much," she sobbed.

Manly tears were running down the husband's cheeks. "It was all my fault, girlie," he said.

"No! no!" she cried, "the fault was mine. I was little, mean, and jealous; and oh! the shame of it. I was jealous of my own daughter."

"Hush, Virgie," commanded the husband. "I should have been more of a man. My love and sympathy should have made me understand. I

Salem Tutt Whitney

was conceited; you wounded my pride and vanity, and I left you—left my wife and baby to the mercy of strangers. Virgie," he pleaded, "can you ever forgive me?"

"There is nothing to forgive, Freddie boy," she answered; "we have both been foolish. I was as guilty as you; but what does it matter, since we are together again."

Roused by the sound of voices, Elsie sat up in bed, "Little mother, has papa come?" she asked, drowsily. The father loosened his wife's arms from about his neck, bounded to the bedside and gathered the little girl into his arms, where she nestled affectionately. "I knowed Santa would bring you to me and little mother," she murmured.

"He didn't forget to send the dolly," said the mother, as she held it before Elsie's wondering eyes.

Just then the clock in the tower began to strike the midnight hour. Immediately the Trinity chimes began to ring out the melody of that wonderful hymn, "All hail the power of Jesus' name." While the beautiful tones echoed and vibrated upon the midnight air, they three stood with arms entwined about each other. After the last sweet strain had whispered itself away into the silence of the winter night, the father said, "It is Christmas now, little Lady."

"God is very good," murmured the mother.

"So is Santa Claus," whispered Elsie.

Bro'r Abr'm Jimson's Wedding: A Christmas Story

PAULINE E. HOPKINS

Pauline E. Hopkins

Widely known as a writer, editor, playwright, singer, and actress, Pauline Elizabeth Hopkins was born in Portland, Maine, in 1859 to William A. and Sarah Allen Hopkins. As the great-grandniece of poet James Whitfield, Pauline was steeped in black middle-class life and culture. However, her exposure to and intimate knowledge of the folklore, lifestyles, and speech patterns of southern black migrants, many of whom belonged to the Baptist and Methodist churches in Boston, provided her with ample material for her novels, short stories, plays, and nonfiction works. Hopkins, a pioneering author, was exceptionally gifted and prolific. Her familiarity with black accomplishments, racial movements, and issues is manifested in her writing.

Frances Ellen Watkins Harper and Pauline Hopkins, among the best-known writers of their time, used their fiction to celebrate the rich cultural history and values of black Americans, and to counter the negative images of blacks and women. As the editor of the *Colored American Magazine,* published in Boston from 1902 to 1904,

Hopkins was specific about the purposes of fiction. In her preface to her first novel, *Contending Forces* (1900), she states that black writers must use fiction to preserve African-American memories. "It is a record of growth and development from generation to generation. *No one will do this for us: we must ourselves develop the men and women who will faithfully portray the inmost thoughts and feelings of the Negro with all the fire and romance which lie dormant in our history.*"

Hopkins was rediscovered by Ann Allen Schockley (*Phylon,* 1972). Her novels, all of which were serialized in the *Colored American Magazine,* include *Contending Forces: A Romance Illustrative of Negro Life North and South* (1900), *Hagar's Daughter: A Story of Southern Caste Prejudice* (1901–1902), and *Winona: A Tale of Negro Life in the South and Southwest* (1902). "Bro'r Abr'm Jimson's Wedding: A Christmas Story" and six of her short stories were published in the *Colored American Magazine.*

"Bro'r Abr'm Jimson's Wedding," published in 1901, contains significant social commentary on the life of African Americans in New England during the latter part of the nineteenth century. Set in the North, in what Hopkins refers to as "B."—most likely Boston, where she spent most of her life—the story is dominated by the powerful presence of three women, Chocolate Caramel Johnson, the widow Maria Nash, and Jane Jimson, and one man, Abraham Jimson. The story presents a rare and penetratingly realistic view of African-

American folk life and culture. Although Hopkins's novels generally focused on the southern elite and upper middle class, in "Bro'r Abr'm Jimson's Wedding" she chooses to focus on working-class blacks with aspirations for middle-class status.

They live in a "populous New England city" where African Americans are "well-to-do" and are extremely concerned about their image. The community values status, hard work, piety, Christian character, honesty, and social commitment.

During the late nineteenth century the church was a powerful force in the lives of black Americans. It was the center of black community life. Most community activities were held in the church, which is where this story begins.

Bro'r Abr'm Jimson's Wedding: A Christmas Story

❧✦❧

It was a Sunday in early spring the first time that Caramel Johnson dawned on the congregation of —— Church in a populous New England city.

The Afro-Americans of that city are well-to-do, being of a frugal nature, and considering it a lasting disgrace for any man among them, desirous of social standing in the community, not to make himself comfortable in this world's goods against the coming time, when old age creeps on apace and renders him unfit for active business.

Therefore the members of the said church had not waited to be exhorted by reformers to own their unpretentious homes and small farms outside the city limits, but they vied with each other in efforts to accumulate a small competency urged thereto by a realization of what pressing needs the future might bring, or it might have been because of the constant example of white neighbors, and a due respect for the dignity which their foresight had brought to the superior race.

Of course, these small Vanderbilts and Astors of a darker hue must have a place of worship in accordance with their worldly prosperity, and so it fell out that ———— church was the richest plum in the ecclesiastical pudding, and greatly sought by scholarly divines as a resting place for four years,—the extent of the time limit allowed by conferences to the men who must be provided with suitable charges according to the demands of their energy and scholarship.

The attendance was unusually large for morning service, and a restless movement was noticeable all through the sermon. How strange a thing is nature; the change of the seasons announces itself in all humanity as well as in the trees and flowers, the grass, and in the atmosphere. Something within us responds instantly to the touch of kinship that dwells in all life.

The air, soft and balmy, laden with rich promise for the future, came through the massive, half-open windows, stealing in refreshing waves upon the congregation. The sunlight fell through the colored glass of the windows in prismatic hues, and dancing all over the lofty star-gemmed ceiling, painted the hue of the broad vault of heaven, creeping down in crinkling shadows to touch the deep garnet cushions of the sacred desk, and the rich wood of the altar with a hint of gold.

The offertory was ended. The silvery cadences of a rich soprano voice still lingered on the air, "O, Worship the Lord in the beauty of holiness." There was a suppressed feeling of expectation, but not the faintest rustle as the minister rose in the pulpit, and after a solemn pause, gave the usual invitation:

  Pauline E. Hopkins

"If there is anyone in this congregation desiring to unite with this church, either by letter or on probation, please come forward to the altar."

The words had not died upon his lips when a woman started from her seat near the door and passed up the main aisle. There was a sudden commotion on all sides. Many heads were turned — it takes so little to interest a church audience. The girls in the choir-box leaned over the rail, nudged each other and giggled, while the men said to one another, "She's a stunner, and no mistake."

The candidate for membership, meanwhile, had reached the altar railing and stood before the man of God, to whom she had handed her letter from a former Sabbath home, with head decorously bowed as became the time and the holy place. There was no denying the fact that she was a pretty girl; brown of skin, small of feature, with an ever-lurking gleam of laughter in eyes coal black. Her figure was slender and beautifully molded, with a seductive grace in the undulating walk and erect carriage. But the chief charm of the sparkling dark face lay in its intelligence, and the responsive play of facial expression which was enhanced by two mischievous dimples pressed into the rounded cheeks by the caressing fingers of the god of love.

The minister whispered to the candidate, coughed, blew his nose on his snowy clerical handkerchief, and, finally, turned to the expectant congregation:

"Sister Chocolate Caramel Johnson—"

He was interrupted by a snicker and a suppressed laugh, again from the choir-box, and an audible whisper which sounded distinctly throughout the quiet church, —

"I'd get the Legislature to change that if it was mine, 'deed I would!" Then silence profound caused by the reverend's stern glance of reproval bent on the offenders in the choir-box.

"Such levity will not be allowed among the members of the choir. If it occurs again, I shall ask the choir master for the names of the offenders and have their places taken by those more worthy to be gospel singers."

Thereupon Mrs. Tilly Anderson whispered to Mrs. Nancy Tobias that, "them choir gals is the mos' deceivines' hussies in the church, an' for my part, I'm glad the pastor called 'em down. That sister's too good lookin' fer 'em, an' they'll be after her like er pack o' houn's, min' me, Sis' Tobias."

Sister Tobias ducked her head in her lap and shook her fat sides in laughing appreciation of the sister's foresight.

Order being restored the minister proceeded:

"Sister Chocolate Caramel Johnson brings a letter to us from our sister church in Nashville, Tennessee. She has been a member in good standing for ten years, having been received into fellowship at ten years of age. She leaves them now, much to their regret, to pursue the study of music at one of the large conservatories in this city, and they recommend her to our love and care. You know the contents of the letter. All in favor of giving Sister Johnson the right hand of fellowship, please manifest the same by a rising vote." The whole congregation rose.

  Pauline E. Hopkins

"Contrary minded? None. The ayes have it. Be seated, friends. Sister Johnson it gives me great pleasure to receive you into this church. I welcome you to its joys and sorrows. May God bless you. Brother Jimson?" (Brother Jimson stepped from his seat to the pastor's side.) "I assign this sister to your class. Sister Johnson, this is Brother Jimson, your future spiritual teacher."

Brother Jimson shook the hand of his new member, warmly, and she returned to her seat. The minister pronounced the benediction over the waiting congregation; the organ burst into richest melody. Slowly the crowd of worshippers dispersed.

Abraham Jimson had made his money as a janitor for the wealthy people of the city. He was a bachelor, and when reproved by some good Christian brother for still dwelling in single blessedness always offered as an excuse that he had been too busy to think of a wife, but that now he was "well fixed," pecuniarily, he would begin to "look over" his lady friends for a suitable companion.

He owned a house in the suburbs and a fine brick dwelling-house in the city proper. He was a trustee of prominence in the church; in fact, its "solid man," and his opinion was sought and his advice acted upon by his associates on the Board. It was felt that any lady in the congregation would be proud to know herself his choice.

When Caramel Johnson received the right hand of fellowship, her aunt, the widow Maria Nash, was ahead in the race for the wealthy class-leader. It had been neck-and-neck for a while between her and

Sister Viney Peters, but, finally it had settled down to Sister Maria with a hundred to one, among the sporting members of the Board, that she carried off the prize, for Sister Maria owned a house adjoining Brother Jimson's in the suburbs, and property counts these days.

Sister Nash had "no idea" when she sent for her niece to come to B. that the latter would prove a rival; her son Andy was as good as engaged to Caramel. But it is always the unexpected that happens. Caramel came, and Brother Jimson had no eyes for the charms of other women after he had gazed into her coal black orbs, and watched her dimples come and go.

Caramel decided to accept a position as housemaid in order to help defray the expenses of her tuition at the conservatory. Brother Jimson interested himself so warmly in her behalf that she soon had a situation in the home of his richest patron where it was handy for him to chat with her about the business of the church, and the welfare of her soul, in general. Things progressed very smoothly until the fall, when one day Sister Maria had occasion to call, unexpectedly, on her niece and found Brother Jimson basking in her smiles while he enjoyed a sumptuous dinner of roast chicken and fixings.

To say that Sister Maria was "set way back" would not accurately describe her feelings; but from that time Abraham Jimson knew that he had a secret foe in the Widow Nash.

  Pauline E. Hopkins

Before many weeks had passed it was publicly known that Brother Jimson would lead Caramel Johnson to the altar "come Christmas." There was much sly speculation as to the "widder's gittin' left," and how she took it from those who had cast hopeless glances toward the chief man of the church. Great preparations were set on foot for the wedding festivities. The bride's trousseau was a present from the groom and included a white satin wedding gown and a costly gold watch. The town house was refurnished and a trip to New York was in contemplation.

"Hump!" grunted Sister Nash when told the rumors, "there's no fool like an ol' fool. Car'mel's a han'ful he'll fin', ef he gits her."

"I reckon he'll git her all right, Sis' Nash," laughed the neighbor, who had run in to talk over the news.

"I've said my word an' I ain't goin' change it, Sis'r. Min' me, I says, *ef he gits her*; an, I mean it."

Andy Nash was also a member of Brother Jimson's class; he possessed, too, a strong sweet baritone voice which made him of great value to the choir. He was an immense success in the social life of the city, and had created sad havoc with the hearts of the colored girls; he could have his pick of the best of them because of his graceful figure and fine easy manners. Until Caramel had been dazzled by the wealth of her elderly lover, she had considered herself fortunate as the lady of his choice.

It was Sunday, three weeks before the wedding that Andy resolved to have it out with Caramel.

"She's been hot an' sh's been col', an' now she's luke warm, an' today ends it befoe this gent-man sleeps," he told himself as he stood before the glass and tied his pale blue silk tie in a stunning knot, and settled his glossy tile [hat] at a becoming angle.

Brother Jimson's class was a popular one and had a large membership; the hour spent there was much enjoyed, even by visitors. Andy went into the vestry early, resolved to meet Caramel if possible. She was there, at the back of the room sitting alone on a settee. Andy immediately seated himself in the vacant place by her side. There were whispers and much head-shaking among the few early worshippers, all of whom knew the story of the young fellow's romance and his disappointment.

As he dropped into the seat beside her, Caramel turned her large eyes on him intently, speculatively, with a doubtful sort of curiosity suggested in her expression, as to how he took her flagrant desertion.

"Howdy, Car'mel?" was his greeting without a shade of resentment.

"I'm well; no need to ask how you are," was the quick response. There was a mixture of cordiality and coquetry in her manner. Her eyes narrowed and glittered under lowered lids, as she gave him a long side-glance. How could she help showing her admiration for the supple young giant beside her? "Surely," she told herself, "I'll have long

   Pauline E. Hopkins

time enough to git sick of old rheumatics," her pet name for her elderly lover.

"I ain't sick much," was Andy's surly reply.

He leaned his elbow on the back of the settee and gave his recreant sweetheart a flaming glance of mingled love and hate, oblivious to the presence of the assembled class-members.

"You ain't over friendly these days, Car'mel, but I gits news of your capers 'roun' 'bout some of the members."

"My—Yes?" she answered as she flashed her great eyes at him in pretended surprise. He laughed a laugh not good to hear.

"Yes," he drawled. Then he added with sudden energy, "Are you goin' to tie up to old Rheumatism sure 'nuff, come Chris'mas?"

"Come Chris'mas, Andy, I be. I hate to tell you but I have to do it."

He recoiled as from a blow. As for the girl, she found a keen relish in the situation; it flattered her vanity.

"How comes it you've changed your mind, Car'mel, 'bout you an' me? You've tol' me often that I was your first choice."

"We—ll," she drawled, glancing uneasily about her and avoiding her aunt's gaze, which she knew was bent upon her every movement, "I did reckon once I would. But a man with money suits me best, an' you ain't got a cent."

"No more have you. You ain't no better than other women to work an' help a man along, is you?"

The color flamed an instant in her face turning the dusky skin to a deep, dull red.

"Andy Nash, you always was a fool, an' as ignerunt as a wil' Injun. I mean to have a sure nuff brick house an' plenty of money. That makes people respec' you. Why don' you quit bein' so shifless and save your money. You ain't worth your salt."

"Your head's turned with pianorer-playin' an' livin' up North. Ef you'll turn *him* off an' come back home, I'll turn over a new leaf, Car'mel," his voice was soft and persuasive enough now.

She had risen to her feet; her eyes flashed, her face was full of pride.

"I won't. I've quit likin' you, Andy Nash."

"Are you in earnest?" he asked, also rising from his seat.

"Dead earnes'."

"Then there's no more to be said."

He spoke calmly, not raising his voice above a whisper. She stared at him in surprise. Then he added as he swung on his heel preparatory to leaving her:

"You ain't got him yet, my gal. But remember, I'm waitin' for you when you need me."

While this whispered conference was taking place in the back part of the vestry, Brother Jimson had entered, and many an anxious glance he cast in the direction of the couple. Andy made his way slowly to his mother's side as Brother Jimson rose in his place to open the meeting. There was a commotion on all sides as the members rustled down on their knees for prayer. Widow Nash whispered to her son as they knelt side by side:

"How did you make out, Andy?"

"Didn't make out at all, mammy; she's as obstinate as a mule."

"Well then, there's only one thing mo' to do."

Andy was unpleasant company for the remainder of the day. He sought, but found nothing to palliate Caramel's treachery. He had only surly, bitter words for his companions who ventured to address him, as the outward expression of inward tumult. The more he brooded over his wrongs the worse he felt. When he went to work on Monday morning he was feeling vicious. He had made up his mind to do something desperate. The wedding should not come off. He would be avenged.

Andy went about his work at the hotel in gloomy silence unlike his usual gay hilarity. It happened that all the female help at the great hostelry was white, and on that particular Monday morning it was the duty of Bridget McCarthy's watch to clean the floors. Bridget was also not in the best of humors, for Pat McClosky, her special company, had gone to the priest with her rival, Kate Connerton, on Sunday afternoon, and Bridget had not yet got over the effects of a strong rum punch taken to quiet her nerves after hearing the news.

Bridget had scrubbed a wide swath of the marble floor when Andy came through with a rush order carried in scientific style high above his head, balanced on one hand. Intent upon satisfying the guest who was princely in his "tips," Andy's unwary feet became entangled in the maelstrom of brooms, scrubbing-brushes and pails. In an instant the "order" was sliding over the floor in a general mix-up.

To say Bridget was mad wouldn't do her state justice. She forgot herself and her surroundings and relieved her feelings in elegant Irish, ending a tirade of abuse by calling Andy a "wall-eyed, bandy-legged nagur."

Andy couldn't stand that from "common, po' white trash," so calling all his science into play he struck out straight from the shoulder with his right, and brought her a swinging blow on the mouth, which seated her neatly in the five-gallon bowl of freshly made lobster salad which happened to be standing on the floor behind her.

There was a wail from the kitchen force that reached to every department. It being the busiest hour of the day when they served dinner, the dish-washers and scrubbers went on a strike against the "nagur who struck Bridget McCarthy, the baste," mingled with cries of "lynch him!" Instantly the great basement floor was a battle ground. Every colored man seized whatever was handiest and ranged himself by Andy's side, and stood ready to receive the onslaught of the Irish brigade. For the sake of peace, and sorely against his inclinations, the proprietor surrendered Andy to the police on a charge of assault and battery.

On Wednesday morning of that eventful week, Brother Jimson wended his way to his house in the suburbs to collect the rent. Unseen by the eye of man, he was wrestling with a problem that had shadowed

    Pauline E. Hopkins

his life for many years. No one on earth suspected him unless it might be the widow. Brother Jimson boasted of his consistent Christian life—rolled his piety like a sweet morsel beneath his tongue, and had deluded himself into thinking that *he* could do no sin. There were scoffers in the church who doubted the genuineness of his pretensions, and he believed that there was a movement on foot against his power led by Widow Nash.

Brother Jimson groaned in bitterness of spirit. His only fear was that he might be parted from Caramel. If he lost her he felt that all happiness in life was over for him, and anxiety gave him a sickening feeling of unrest. He was tormented, too, by jealousy; and when he was called upon by Andy's anxious mother to rescue her son from the clutches of the law, he had promised her fair enough, but in reality resolved to do nothing but—tell the judge that Andy was a dangerous character whom it was best to quell by severity. The pastor and all the other influential members of the church were at court on Tuesday, but Brother Jimson was conspicuous by his absence.

Today Brother Jimson resolved to call on Sister Nash, and, as he had heard nothing of the outcome of the trial, make cautious inquiries concerning that, and also sound her on the subject nearest his heart.

He opened the gate and walked down the side path to the back door. From within came the rhythmic sound of a rubbing board. The brother knocked, and then cleared his throat with a preliminary cough.

"Come," called a voice within. As the door swung open it revealed the spare form of the widow, who with sleeves rolled above her elbows stood at the tub cutting her way through piles of foaming suds.

"Mornin', Sis' Nash! How's all?"

"That you, Bro'r Jimson? How's yourself? Take a cheer an' make yourself to home."

"Cert'nly, Sis' Nash; don' care ef I do," and the good brother scanned the sister with an eagle eye. "Yas'm, I'm purty tol'rable these days, thank God. Bleeg'd to you, sister, I jes' will stop an' res' myself befo' I repair myself back to the city." He seated himself in the most comfortable chair in the room, tilted it on the two back legs against the wall, lit his pipe and with a grunt of satisfaction settled back to watch the white rings of smoke curl about his head.

"These are mighty ticklish times, Sister. How's you continue on the journey? Is you strong in the faith?"

"I've got the faith, my brother, but I ain't on no mountain top this week. I'm way down in the valley; I'm jes' coaxin' the Lord to keep me sweet," and Sister Nash wiped the ends from her hands and prodded the clothes in the boiler with the clothes-stick, added fresh pieces and went on with her work.

"This is a worl' strewed with wrecks and flotin' with tears. It's the valley of tribulation. May your faith continue. I hear Jim Jinkins has bought a farm up Taunton way."

"Wan'ter know!"

"Doctor tells me Bro'r Waters is comin' after Chris-mus. They do say as how he's stirrin' up things turrible; he's easin' his min' on this lynchin' business, an' it's high time—high time."

"Sho! Don' say so! What you reck'n he's gon' tell us now, Brother Jimson?"

"Suthin' stonishin', Sister; it'll stir the country from end to end. Yes'm, the Council is powerful strong as an organ'zation."

"Sho! sho!" and the "thrub, thrub" of the board could be heard a mile away.

The conversation flagged. Evidently Widow Nash was not in a talkative mood that morning. The brother was disappointed.

"Well, it's mighty comfort'ble here, but I mus' be goin'."

"What's your hurry, Brother Jimson?"

"Business, Sister, business," and the brother brought his chair forward preparatory to rising. "Where's Andy? How'd he come out of that little difficulty?"

"Locked up."

"You don' mean to say he's in jail?"

"Yes; he's in jail 'tell I git's his bail."

"What might the sentence be, Sister?"

"Twenty dollars fine or six months at the Islan'." There was silence for a moment, broken only by the "thrub, thrub" of the washboard, while the smoke curled upward from Brother Jimson's pipe as he enjoyed a few last puffs.

"These are mighty ticklish times, Sister. Po' Andy, the way of the transgressor is hard."

Sister Nash took her hands out of the tub and stood with arms akimbo, a statue of Justice carved in ebony. Her voice was like the trump of doom.

"Yes; an' men like you is the cause of it. You leadin' men with money an' chances don' do your duty. I arst you, I arst you fair, to go down to the jedge an' bail that po' chile out. Did you go? No; you hard-faced old devil, you lef him be there, an' I had to git the money from my white folks. Yes, an' I'm breakin' my back now, over that pile of clo's to pay that twenty dollars. Um! all the trouble comes to us women."

"That's so, Sister; that the livin' truth," murmured Brother Jimson furtively watching the rising storm and wondering where the lightning of her speech would strike next.

"I tell you what it is our receiptfulness to each other is the reason we don' prosper an' God's a-punishin' us with fire an' with sward 'cause we's so jealous an' snaky to each other."

"That's so, Sister; that's the livin' truth."

"Yes, sir, a nigger's boun' to be a nigger 'tell the trump of doom. You kin skin him, but he's a nigger still. Broadcloth, biled shirts an' money won' make him more or less, no, sir."

"That's so, Sister; that's jes' so."

"A nigger can't holp himself. White folks can run agin the law all the time an' they never gits caught, but a nigger! Every time he opens his mouth he puts his foot in it—got to hit that po' white trash gal in the mouth an' git jailed, an' leave his po'r ol' mother to work her fingers to the secon' jint to git him out. Um!"

"These are mighty ticklish times, Sister. Man's boun' to sin; it's his nat'ral state. I hope this will teach Andy humility of the sperit."

"A little humility'd be good for yourself, Abr'm Jimson." Sister Nash ceased her sobs and set her teeth hard.

"Lord, Sister Nash, what compar'son is there 'twixt me an' a worthless nigger like Andy? My business is with the salt of the earth, an' so I have dwelt ever since I was consecrated."

"Salt of the earth! But ef the salt have los' its saver how you goin' salt it ergin'? No, sir, you cain't do it; it mus be cas' out an' trodded under foot of men. That's who's goin' happen you Abe Jimson, hyar me? An' I'd like to trod on you with my foot, an' every ol' good fer nutin bag o' salt like you," shouted Sister Nash. "You're a snake in the grass; you done stole the boy's gal an' then try to git him sent to the Islan'. You cain't deny it, fer the jedge done tol' me all you said, you ol' rhinoceros-hided hypercrite. Salt of the earth! You!"

Brother Jimson regretted that Widow Nash had found him out. Slowly he turned, settling his hat on the back of his head.

"Good mornin', Sister Nash. I ain't no hard feelin's agains' you. I'm too near to the kindom to let trifles jar me. My bowels of compassion yearns over you, Sister, a pilgrim an' a stranger in this unfriendly worl'."

No answer from Sister Nash. Brother Jimson lingered.

"Good mornin', Sister," still no answer.

"I hope to see you at the weddin', Sister."

"Keep on hopin' I'll be there. That gal's my own sister's chile. What in time she wants of a rheumatic ol' sap-head like you for, beats me. I wouldn't marry you for no money, myself; no, sir; it's my belief that you've done goophered her."

"Yes, Sister; I've hearn tell of people refusin' befo' they was ask'd," he retorted, giving her a sly look.

For answer the widow grabbed the clothes-stick and flung it at him in speechless rage.

"My, what a temper it's got," remarked Brother Jimson soothingly as he dodged the shovel, the broom, the coal-hod and the stove-covers. But he sighed with relief as he turned into the street and caught the faint sound of the washboard now resumed.

To a New Englander the season of snow and ice with its clear biting atmosphere, is the ideal time for the great festival. Christmas morning dawned in royal splendor; the sun kissed the snowy streets and turned the icicles into brilliant stalactites. The bells rang a joyous call from every steeple, and soon the churches were crowded with eager worshippers—

eager to hear again the oft-repeated, the wonderful story on which the heart of the whole Christian world feeds its faith and hope. Words of tender faith, marvelous in their simplicity fell from the lips of a world renowned preacher, and touched the hearts of the listening multitude:

"The winter sunshine is not more bright and clear than the atmosphere of living joy, which stretching back between our eyes and that picture of Bethlehem, shows us its beauty in unstained freshness. And as we open once again those chapters of the gospel in which the ever fresh and living picture stands, there seems from year to year always to come some newer, brighter meaning into the words that tell the tale.

"St. Matthew says that when Jesus was born in Bethlehem the wise men came from the East to Jerusalem. The East means man's search after God; Jerusalem means God's search after man. The East means the religion of the devout soul; Jerusalem means the religion of the merciful God. The East means Job's cry, 'Oh, that I knew where I might find him!' Jerusalem means 'Immanuel-God with us.'"

Then the deep-toned organ joined the grand chorus of human voices in a fervent hymn of praise and thanksgiving:

> *"Lo! the Morning Star appeareth,*
> *O'er the world His beams are cast;*
> *He the Alpha and Omega,*
> *He, the Great, the First the Last!*

Hallelujah! hallelujah!
Let the heavenly portal ring!
Christ is born, the Prince of glory!
Christ the Lord, Messiah, King!"

Everyone of prominence in church circles had been bidden to the Jimson wedding. The presents were many and costly. Early after service on Christmas morning the vestry rooms were taken in hand by leading sisters to prepare the tables for the supper, for on account of the host of friends bidden to the feast, the reception was to be held in the vestry.

The tables groaned beneath their loads of turkey, salads, pies, puddings, cakes and fancy ices.

Yards and yards of evergreen wreaths encircled the granite pillars; the altar was banked with potted plants and cut flowers. It was a beautiful sight. The main aisle was roped off for the invited guests, with white satin ribbons.

Brother Jimson's patrons were to be present in a body, and they had sent the bride a solid silver service, so magnificent that the sisters could only sigh with envy.

The ceremony was to take place at seven sharp. Long before that hour the ushers in full evening dress, were ready to receive the guests. Sister Maria Nash was among the first to arrive, and even the Queen of Sheba was not arrayed like unto her. At fifteen minutes before the hour, the organist began an elaborate instrumental performance. There was an expectant hush and much head-turning when the music changed to the familiar strains of the "Wedding March." The minister took his place inside the railing ready to receive the party. The groom waited at the altar.

First came the ushers, then the maids of honor, then the flower girl—daughter of a prominent member—carrying a basket of flowers which she scattered before the bride, who was on the arm of the best man. In the bustle and confusion incident to the entrance of the wedding party no one noticed a group of strangers accompanied by Andy Nash, enter and occupy seats near the door.

The service began. All was quiet. The pastor's words fell clearly upon the listening ears. He had reached the words:

"If any man can show just cause," etc., when like a thunder-clap came a voice from the back part of the house—an angry excited voice, and a woman of ponderous avoirdupois advanced up the aisle.

"Hol' on thar, pastor, hol'on! A man cain't have but one wife 'cause it's agin' the law. I'm Abe Jimson's lawful wife, an' hyars his six children—all boys—to pint out their daddy." In an instant the assembly was in confusion.

"My soul," exclaimed Viney Peters, "the ol' sarpen'! An' to think how near I come to takin' up with him. I'm glad I ain't Car'mel."

Sis'r Maria said nothing, but a smile of triumph lit up her countenance.

"Brother Jimson, is this true?" demanded the minister, sternly. But Abraham Jimson was past answering. His face was ashen, his teeth chattering, his hair standing on end. His shaking limbs refused to uphold his weight; he sank upon his knees on the steps of the altar.

But now a hand was laid upon his shoulder and Mrs. Jimson hauled him upon his feet with a jerk.

"Abe Jimson, you know me. You run'd way from me up North fifteen year ago, an' you hid yourself like a groun' hog in a hole, but I've got you. Ther'll be no new wife in the Jimson family this week. I'm yer fus' wife an' I'll be yer las' one. Git up hyar now, you mis'able sinner an' tell the pastor who I be." Brother Jimson meekly obeyed the clarion voice. His sanctified air had vanished; his pride humbled into the dust.

"Pastor," came in trembling tones from his quivering lips. "These are mighty ticklish times." He paused. A deep silence followed his words. "I'm a weakkneed, mis'able sinner. I have fallen under temptation. This is Ma' Jane, my wife, an' these hyar boys is my sons, God forgive me."

The bride, who had been forgotten now, broke in:

"Abraham Jimson, you ought to be hung. I'm goin' to sue you for breach of promise." It was a fatal remark. Mrs. Jimson turned upon her.

"You will, will you? Sue him, will you? I'll make a choc'late Car'mel of you befo' I'm done with you, you 'ceitful hussy, hoodooin' hones' men from thar wives."

  Pauline E. Hopkins

She sprang upon the girl, tearing, biting, rendering. The satin gown and gossamer veil were reduced to rags, Caramel emitted a series of ear-splitting shrieks, but the biting and tearing went on. How it might have ended no one can tell if Andy had not sprang over the backs of the pews and grappled with the infuriated woman.

The excitement was intense. Men and women struggled to get out of the church. Some jumped from the windows and others crawled under the pews, where they were secure from violence. In the midst of the melee, Brother Jimson disappeared and was never seen again, and Mrs. Jimson came into possession of his property by due process of law.

In the church Abraham Jimson's wedding and his fall from grace is still spoken of in eloquent whispers.

In the home of Mrs. Andy Nash a motto adorns the parlor walls worked in scarlet wool and handsomely framed in gilt. The text reads: "Ye are the salt of the earth; there is nothing hidden that shall not be revealed."

Two Christmas Days:
A Holiday Story

IDA WELLS BARNETT

Ida Wells Barnett

Ida Wells Barnett, called "the Princess of the Press," was widely known as an editor, journalist, lecturer, social reformer, and feminist. She was born enslaved on July 16, 1862, at Holly Springs, Mississippi. The death of her parents during the yellow fever epidemic of 1878 left her and her five brothers and sisters to fend for themselves. Ida, determined to keep the family together, assumed the responsibility of raising her siblings. She attended Rust College in her hometown, a Freedmen's Aid school, which like many other black colleges was a normal school with all grade levels. She passed the examination for county schoolteacher and received an appointment to teach in a one-room school. She later moved to Memphis, Tennessee, where she taught for seven years in the Memphis school system. It was during this time that she attended summer school at Fisk University and studied privately with several accomplished teachers. In 1895, she married attorney Ferdinand Barnett, a widower.

Wells Barnett's talent as a writer became evident during her editorship of the *Evening Star*, a church paper. Her success as editor led to an invitation to write for the *Living Way,* a Baptist weekly. Writing under the pen name "Iola" she wrote an article on a railroad suit she had brought against the Chesapeake & Ohio Railroad. This was the beginning of Wells Barnett's lifelong public campaign against the injustices faced by African Americans. Her early journalistic efforts were highly successful, opening up opportunities for her to write for the *American Baptist, Detroit Plaindealer, Christian Index, A.M.E. Zion Church Review, Indianapolis World, New York Age,* and many other publications. In 1889, she became the first black woman to attend the Afro-American Press Convention in Louisville, Kentucky, and was elected assistant secretary. During that same year, she bought a one-third interest in the Memphis *Free Speech and Headlight.* Her critique of the poor conditions of the local black schools caused her dismissal from her teaching position. Her paper was later destroyed by an angry white mob, who reacted to a blistering editorial she wrote in which she condemned the lynching of three black businessmen. She urged blacks to boycott white businesses and to leave Memphis for the West. Her partner was run out of town, and whites threatened to kill her. The editorial in dispute alleged that "nobody in this section believes the old thread-bare lie that Negro men assault white women. If southern white men are not careful they will over-reach themselves and a conclusion will be reached which will be very damaging to the moral reputation of their women."

Exiled from Memphis, Wells Barnett was invited by T. Thomas Fortune to write for the *New York Age.* Her first article, published on

June 25, 1892, was a front-page piece on lynching. In October of that year, it was published in pamphlet form and called "Southern Horrors: Lynch Law in All Its Phases." Wells Barnett's militant writings against lynching brought her fame and led to numerous speaking engagements and a tour of England, Scotland, and Wales in 1893–1894. Her efforts led to the formation of the British Anti-Lynching Committee. In 1895, Wells Barnett published *A Red Record: Tabulated Statistics and Alleged Causes of Lynching in the United States, 1892–1893–1894,* a historical and statistical study of lynching.

Although Wells Barnett is best known for her militant writings against lynching, she also wrote articles that criticized what she viewed as the hypocrisy of the black intellectual elite. During her long and fruitful life, she was opposed by whites and as frequently by blacks, particularly some black men who questioned a woman assuming a role as key spokesperson for the race on a major issue. Black women also exhibited hostility toward Wells Barnett, by frequently criticizing her motives.

In 1894, she published the short story "Two Christmas Days: A Holiday Story," which appears to be partly autobiographical. The work is full of insights into black middle- and upper-class life in the 1890s and its worldview. Wells Barnett portrays life among the black middle class, where black professionals struggle to achieve and rise above the legacy of slavery in an environment that is hostile to their very being. This group was concerned about the pervasiveness of racism in American life. A central theme in this story focuses attention on the need for black professionals to dedicate their lives to racial uplift. The story also addresses temperance and migration.

This story centers on Emily Minton, a twenty-three-year-old graduate of a southern black college, who is independent, confident, highly competitive, determined, and committed to the uplift of the black community. Emily, similar to Wells Barnett, is concerned about the strength of black men and the need for them as professionals to be exemplary leaders, giving unstinted dedicated service to their race. Her singular focus on black men developing a strong sense of character and assuming a leadership which challenged the status quo and addressed hard issues of racism in America is perhaps the major theme of this story. It is the guiding issue in her life, particularly as relates to choosing a mate.

Wells Barnett also believed that the responsibility of the educated black elite was to the race, and that this value should be factored into everything that one did.

Late-nineteenth-century views of manhood and masculinity assumed that a man would be hard-working, courageous, independent, and responsible. He should chose a profession that would allow him to effect change and make a difference, in particular because he wished to address the African-American condition, not because it paid a lot of money. This ideal was clearly evidenced in Wells Barnett's life. Though she was offered more lucrative teaching positions in the North and West, she chose to teach her people in the South, where she felt the need was greatest.

Two Christmas Days: A Holiday Story

"Going out to Wilsons' this afternoon, George?"

"For what," asks George.

"To the croquet party. You surely haven't forgotten it."

"By George, Harry, I just had. It's too confoundedly hot to do what you have to, much less croquet. But Mrs. Wilson would never forgive me if I didn't go. This affair is in honor of her guest, I believe; Miss— what's her name?"

"Minton. Well if you are going, it's time you're getting a move on you. It's past five now," said Harry, rising.

"Guess I'll have to, as I haven't even called on the young lady yet. It's too bad to have to play the agreeable when you don't want to. Wait a minute, I'll go up with you." And George Harris leisurely put away his law papers, and was soon on the way with his friend, Harry Brown.

Arriving at the home of Mrs. Wilson they found the spacious green lawn alive with young girls in cool summer dresses, who with obliging partners were playing at croquet.

Mrs. Wilson and her son, Clarence, railed the young men on being late and introduced Harris, who knew of but had never met Miss Minton until now.

"What do you think of the visitor, George?" asked his friend as they rested on one of the rustic settees watching the players.

"Don't know," drawled George. "You can't tell much about girls at first sight. One thing she doesn't seem to put on airs. I take it also, that she goes in to win in everything she attempts. She is the only one of all those girls who cares a pin about being beaten. See how hard she works in this heat, and with what precision she makes her shots. The other girls are so taken up with flirting with their partners, they neither know nor care when their turn comes to play."

"Ah, George, at your old professional habit of dissecting every character you meet in that cold analytic fashion. Don't you see anything to admire in the woman?"

"Yes, I see she is charmingly and becomingly dressed—a thing so few girls have the good taste to do."

Harry laughed. "You're a hard critic, my fastidious friend. You'll meet your match yet some day, old fellow; then you'll rave, too, over your lady's charms without stopping to analyze her."

The conversation was ended, as with a peal of laughter Miss Minton and her partner won. Flushed with excitement and victory, she seated herself in the place vacated by Harry Brown, who went to take a hand in another game just beginning. She and George exchanged a few words, and as she rested he looked at her more closely. She was a tall, slender, graceful girl, olive complexion, black hair and eyes. She was not strictly beautiful, but the features were regular and there was a nobility of expression which betokened the thinker; a clear open countenance, with wonderful eyes, a sweet yet dignified manner. Her dress of pink muslin fitted her figure to perfection and suited her complexion admirably. She was twenty-three years old and was a college graduate from one of the American Missionary Colleges in the South. She had made so enviable a record that she was appointed teacher in her Alma Mater—the first Afro-American teacher they had ever employed. She was in high spirits over her victory and her sallies of wit interested the young man beside her. He mentally decided to see more of her.

Meanwhile twilight had fallen and it was too dark to see the wickets. Mrs. Wilson called and the guests gathered round the dining room table, a laughing, happy group. While they discussed melons and ices, they chatted of everything in general and nothing in particular, as young folks will.

"So you have really decided to go to Oklahoma, Will," asked Mrs. Wilson, during a lull in the gay badinage.

"Yes, ma'am," replied Will Bramlette, a tall brown-skinned young fellow of twenty-five. "I leave next week."

"But I can't see what you want to go away out there for; you are doing well here at your trade. Mr. Wilson says you have all the work you can do."

"Yes, but I want to do better. I want to live where I can have something, and a man is as free as anybody else, once in my life. If Uncle Sam will give me one hundred and sixty acres of land to go and get it, I'm going after it sure."

"Oklahoma will never see me," laughed one of the young men. "Nor me," echoed another.

"I admire your spirit and determination, Mr. Bramlette," said Emily Minton, speaking very quickly.

"What, you an Oklahoma convert too?" chorused a number of voices.

"Yes, I am. I have long thought our young men have not enough ambition and get-up, or they couldn't be content to drift along here in the South the way things are going every day. For the last half dozen years, ever since I've been able to see clearly the causes of so much race trouble, everybody has said education would solve the problem. I have watched the young men who have left school when I was a pupil and since I became a teacher. They gave signs of the brightest promise, but the majority soon fall into a soft easy position which affords them a living and there they vegetate, until they lose all the manhood they ever possessed. If I could have my way with them, I'd transplant them all to

Oklahoma or some place else where they would have to work and that would develop character and strengthen manhood in them."

"Thank you, Miss Emily, for your endorsement," said Will Bramlette. "It has given me a better determination, as the Methodist sisters say."

"Are you not rather hard on the young men, Miss Minton?" asked George Harris.

"I think not," she answered; "the race needs their services so much. Indeed, I think the most discouraging feature of it all, is the seeming contentment under conditions which ought to stir all the manhood's blood in them. So whenever I do meet one who thinks as I do and is ambitious to be somebody, I cannot help wishing him God-speed. If I were a man, I would join him only too quick."

"You might join him some anyway, Emily," said one of the young girls.

"Yes, indeed, and be far more acceptable as a companion—a help-mate," Mrs. Wilson teasingly rejoined.

Everybody laughed, and even Emily, who had grown very earnest, was forced to smile at this clever turning of the tables on herself.

The party broke up, but George and Harry lingered in the moonlight on the veranda talking to the homefolks. George felt strangely attracted to this girl, and, walking over to where she sat, he said, watching her out of the corners of his eyes: "Bramlette was delighted with your approval of his course, Miss Minton. You have made a conquest of him already. That's the way with you girls—you have no mercy on a fellow's heart. How many scalps have you dangling at your belt already?"

Emily turned on him with a grieved, reproachful expression: "You do not mean to say you think me a flirt, Mr. Harris?"

"No, indeed," he said, quickly dropping his jesting tone, "I think you are too noble a girl for that." George spoke so gravely and respectfully that Emily knew he meant it.

"Thank you," she said simply. He bade them good-night and left shortly after.

"She is a remarkable girl," mused George as he went home. He called the next afternoon and the next. Very soon it so happened that there was no day after the Sun-God hid his face, that George Harris did not "call by" on his way home, although it was several blocks out of his way. Sometimes it was a proposed walk, oftener a drive, a few flowers, or a few minutes conversation. Mrs. Wilson's niece was a brilliant musician, and George had a fine baritone voice, and they made splendid music these long summer evenings. Emily had the soul of a musician, with none of a musician's talent.

Those evenings with the moonlight, the music and the fragrance of the rose, the honeysuckle and the night-blooming jasmine, seemed the happiest of her life. She had become interested in this man as in no other, and she had met many in her short life. But this man with courtly manners, general culture and quiet, yet masterful and self-contained bearing, was unlike any she had ever met. If a day passed without his coming, she was conscious of a something lacking in its pleasure. Given to self-examination, she felt that she was falling in love, and she was sure the interest was mutual. She mentally determined before yielding herself to the fascinations of her feelings, to know more about him. The opportunity came soon after.

While down town shopping one hot August day, they passed Harris's office. Mrs. Wilson teasingly asked Emily if she would like to call on him. She consented and they stepped into the office only to find him absent. The room was such a disagreeable surprise to her, that Emily was glad Harris was absent. It was a dingy apartment, with old and rickety furniture, and the atmosphere was musty with the fumes of tobacco smoke. There was absolutely nothing to harmonize with the careful, cleanly well-dressed man she had known for nearly two months. She gave no sign but was glad when Mrs. Wilson said they would not wait.

At tea-table that evening, the conversation turned on Harris, and Emily inquired of Mr. Wilson how long the young lawyer had been practicing, and was told about five years.

"Do our people patronize him very well? You know it seems our failing never to have the same confidence in our own ability that we have in the white man's," said she.

"I don't think it's our people's fault this time, Miss Emily. We've all known George ever since he was a baby and were proud of his record at school. When he came home and opened an office, I sent him several cases and gave him some of my own work to do. He attended to them all right enough, but he didn't get out and 'hustle' for other work. He's either too proud to do it, or lacks energy, one or the other. We all feel that he's no woman that we should be hunting work for. He gets work enough to do around these magistrate's courts and now and then a case in the Criminal Court, and manages to make a living out of these petty cases, but he's never had a case of any special merit that has demonstrated his real ability, like that young Johnson of your town."

The conversation drifted to other topics, but Emily thought she could understand some things more clearly than before.

A day or so after, in a talk with Harris about mutual friends who had gone out into the world, he was aroused at the trenchant criticism. "How merciless you are toward us poor fellows, Miss Emily," he exclaimed.

"Yes, indeed," she quickly replied. "I have no patience with dawdlers."

"But you find fault with all. Are there none who merit your ladyship's favor?"

"If not, it is because they do not measure up to their highest possibilities," she said.

"No? Well you shouldn't expect them to do so at a bound."

"But so few seem to be even striving in that direction, Mr. Harris. That's the discouraging feature. Even Mr. Harris, who might achieve splendid success in his profession—and of course any distinction he

  Ida Wells Barnett

might win, would redound to the credit of his race—does not seem ambitious to do so." She spoke gently yet regretfully.

George was silenced for the moment, but rallying immediately said: "Give us a picture of your model man, Miss Emily?"

"But where would I find a model to sit for the picture?" asked Emily playfully.

"Take me," said George, with double meaning in his tone and a tender light in his eyes.

"You?" asked Emily, striving hard to seem unself-conscious; "you wouldn't do at all—there's one great objection."

"What is it, Emily?" eagerly asked George. "Tell me please."

"Not to-night," she said, shaking her head, "some other time."

George's musings as he walked home that night were not of the most pleasant kind. It was not the first time since he knew this girl that he had left her presence with a faint feeling of discontent with himself and surroundings. He wondered what was the particular flaw this keen-eyed young woman had discovered in his make-up. The thought haunted him all next day and when wending his way homeward to dinner, he spied her in a hammock in the yard. With the liberty of a frequent visitor, he went in, and after a few words, asked her what was the fault she had found in him. She laughed musically, yet there was a tremor in her voice as she railed him about his "woman's curiosity." He persisted, telling her he had thought of it all day.

"Have you not hit upon it yet?"

"I can think of only one thing," said he; "is it that I am not tall enough?"

Emily blushed as she saw he was thinking her objection a personal one. She felt he was on the eve of a proposal and she thought it her duty to spare him the refusal, if possible. She laughed again to cover her embarrassment and asked what height would have to do with the "model man."

"It's a question of deeds, not physical proportions, Mr. Harris," she remarked gravely.

He took her hand and in a voice trembling with emotion, besought her to tell him what it was. She thought a moment. "You promise not to be angry?"

"I promise."

"Well, Mr. Harris, I am almost sorry I spoke," she said, "but since you will have it, if I were asked the principal drawback to your becoming a model man I should say it is a love of—liquor."

He dropped her hand and turned away. After a moment he said in a constrained tone: "May I ask how Miss Minton has become so wise as to my habits?"

"I have detected the smell of it on your breath," answered Emily, flushing as she rapidly continued. "I hope you won't be angry, my friend, but I have wondered that you seem to have so much leisure. I was in your office one day and was struck with the general poverty of your surroundings. Mr. Johnson, of my own town, has as fine an office as there is in the city, and has made a name for successful practice in the Criminal and Chancery courts. He has not your education, nor has he been practicing so long. For a man of such brilliant parts, I thought there must be a reason for such contentment, such a seeming lack of energy. I have concluded this is the reason, but I should not have risked your displeasure by saying so, if you had not urged me. The race needs the best service our young manhood can give it, my friend, and it seems so wrong to divert any part of it to the practice of a habit which can bring you no credit and gratify no noble ambition."

George's mind was in a conflicting whirl of emotions. He knew she spoke the truth; and yet with all his feelings of anger and mortification, he seemed to feel that this peerless girl was slipping away from him. He wanted her to think well of him and forgetful of the French proverb: "He who excuses, accuses," said eagerly:

"But this habit of mine never interferes with my business, Miss Emily. Indeed it rather helps me. I am the only Afro-American at this bar, and I must have stimulus to help me through the difficulties the wall of prejudice throws in my way. Besides had I wished to appear other than I am, I might have kept this knowledge from you."

"But it isn't I, who is to be considered," said Emily, struggling for composure. "It is the race, Mr. Harris, and what you owe it. This habit may not have seriously interfered before, but it will, if indulged, render you less ambitious to excel, if nothing more. For us as a race, in our present position, stagnation means death. The men who are best fitted for it, should be the leaders; those who lead others must be slaves to no unworthy passion or habit. The model man—*my* model man—is in deed and truth, in body and mind, master of himself."

As the low earnest tones ceased to vibrate, Emily extended her hand and George pressed it warmly, saying, "Thank you, Miss Emily. No girl ever talked to me that way before."

"I have paid your common sense a compliment in that I have risked your displeasure to be your friend, and you do not know how I appreciate your manner of taking it," she said. "You know I go away tomorrow, and as you have made the summer so pleasant for me, I should like for us to part friends."

"You will let me write to you?" asked George. She gave her consent and on the morrow went home.

George wrote her before the week was out; throughout the fall he sent her letters regularly telling of his struggles. He understood as fully as if she had told him in so many words, that if he would win her he must make himself worthy, and he manfully withstood the jeers of his friends on his refusal to drink.

Emily answered promptly and rejoiced that the latent forces in him were at last roused to action. Her love for him and faith in him grew stronger with every letter. She looked forward to a promised visit during the holidays with much anticipation.

George arrived in the city New Year's Eve; was met by old friends who had arranged a "stag" for him at the home of the friend with whom he was to stop. He was tempted and yielded for the first time in four months, and drank the more for his past abstinence. In the early morning hours he was helped to bed by the "boys" who all voted him a jolly good fellow.

He arose late the next day with a terrible headache and guilty conscience; he was to call on Emily that afternoon, and he knew she would discover his condition. With a mental comment on being soft enough to defer to a "woman's whim," he obeyed the craving for a "stimulant" and took several drinks during the day. When he presented himself at the house, Emily went forward to meet him with beaming face and outstretched hand, and presented "My friend, Mr. Harris," to the several callers in the room. Catching the smell of liquor, she looked at him searchingly and as she realized his condition felt as if turned to stone. The heat and Emily's constraint, had their effect on George. He talked volubly and loudly, and the fumes of brandy were distilled throughout the room.

Emily maintained her composure till the other guests had gone; then without a word she broke down and wept convulsively. Shame, surprise, indignation and mortification each struggled for the mastery. No one had ever dared to come in her presence in such condition before, and to receive this humiliation at the hands of the man she loved; and in the presence of witnesses to whom she had spoken so highly of him. What must they think of her—Miss Minton, the exclusive? To think that after all these years of choosing, her heart should go out to a—drunkard!

George came and stood before her. "Tears for me, my darling? I am not worthy of them. I came here to ask you to marry me, but after such a weak, miserable spectacle, I know it is useless. I do not deserve even your forgiveness. Farewell." He left the house, and the city that same evening. He wrote Emily a long letter of apology, telling her how dearly he loved her and that her influence could save him from his weakness and make a man of him. He told her how he came to yield to his weakness without sparing himself and cast himself on her mercy.

Emily wept over this letter. Her heart pleaded for the writer, but she could not get the consent of her judgement to risk her happiness in the hands of a man whom she could not trust; who was not master of himself. Though it cost her a great deal to say so, she did it after a night of anguish.

Shortly after, she heard that he had wound up his business suddenly and gone West, and then she heard no more for two years.

One day in November she found a letter on her return from school, in a strange hand writing. It read as follows:

> Oklahoma City, O.T. [Oklahoma Territory],
> Nov. 15, 1892

Dear Miss Minton:

You may not remember me and you must pardon the liberty I take. But for the sake of a friend one risks much. I am the one you so generously encouraged when I declared my intention to come to Oklahoma nearly three years ago. I came and have never regretted it. Nearly two years ago, my friend George Harris joined me and we have been together ever since. In our lonely hours he has talked much of you and I know how dear you are to him. Since that fatal New Year's Day, (you see he has told me all,) not a drop of liquor has passed his lips. He says it lost him the only woman he ever loved and he never wants to look at it again. He thinks you have never forgiven him, and says he doesn't blame you. He has built up a fine practice in the territory by hard work, and now he is very ill with pneumonia. He has the best attention, but he does not care to get well; he has lost all hope and says nothing when he is himself but when he is out of his mind he is always calling your name. He does not know I have written this letter, but I know a word from you would do him more good than medicine.

Won't you write him a word, Miss Emily, and save the best friend I have on earth,

And Oblige, Yours,
WILL BRAMLETTE.

Emily was crying when she finished, but they were happy tears. Without a word she sat down at the desk and this is the letter she sent him:

MY OWN DEAR LOVE:

A little bird has brought me the news that you are a very sick man and that you do not get well because you do not seem to care to live. If I tell you that I wish you to live for my sake, will you try to get well? I have always loved you, and since you would neither write to me nor ask me again to marry you, I am going to make use of my leap year prerogative and ask you to marry me. As the New Year is near at hand, and I have no gift to send, now that I know where you are, I have been wondering if you would accept me as a New Year's gift, and if you will be able to come for me by the New Year. I have a fancy I would like to give myself to you on that day. Will you come?

Yours,
Emily

When Bramlette read this letter to the sick man it was Thanksgiving Day, and tears of thankfulness stole down his wasted cheeks. "Can you pray Will?" he asked. "Then kneel down here and thank God for my happiness." A look of great content spread over his face. "Write her a letter, Will, and tell her I'll be there on New Year's Day if God spares my life."

He called for food and with the precious letter pressed to his heart, he fell asleep with the first smile Will had seen on his face. The letter which had been more than medicine, he had Will read every day until he was able to read it himself, and having something to live for, he gradually got better. Will wrote to Emily every day and she sent loving cheerful messages in return, urging him to be careful of his health. He had never been a demonstrative man, but when he was able to write, he poured out his soul to her and consecrated the life he said she had given back to him, to renewed effort for individual and race advancement. "With you by my side," he wrote, "to cheer life's pathway and strengthen my zeal, life which has been so dreary, will indeed be enriched and ennobled."

Emily handed in her resignation, to take effect with the holidays. On New Year's Day, directly after the service, these two, pronounced the words which for "better or for worse" unite them "until death do us part." Then hand in hand they went out to the boundless West to make a home together, in which love and confidence reign supreme.

A Christmas Party That Prevented a Split in the Church

MARGARET BLACK

Margaret Black

In 1916, John Murphy, the editor of the Baltimore *Afro-American,* described Margaret Black as a "writer and thinker of experience" and "an occasional writer of delightful short stories." Indeed, she was all of this and more. Although we do not know where or when she was born, in 1896 she began her writing career as the editor of the paper's "Women's Column." The initial column, which appears to have lasted for less than a year, reappeared in 1916 and enjoyed a run of at least three years. Published simultaneously with the column were Black's short stories. An outspoken feminist, she announced to her readers that "this column has its limits as well as its purposes. The editor allows us only a short space and being women, of course we must bow to the inevitable." In her writing she addressed a number of issues that reflected the distinct consciousness of black women in the past, a worldview that was distinctive from those of black men and white women.

Black's "Women's Column," as well as her short stories, provides a unique opportunity to discover how black women viewed their society and how they strove to change it. Short stories such as "A Christmas Party That Prevented a Split in the Church" provided a definition of black women's culture, specifically their values, practices, and institutions, and their ways of looking at the world common to a large number of black women in the nineteenth and twentieth centuries who belonged to the church missionary societies. Given the large numbers of working and middle-class women who participated in these organizations, as well as the fact that this was a key base of power for black women, we are able to observe black women's consciousness and culture from a unique vantage point.

"A Christmas Party That Prevented a Split in the Church," published in 1916, is a story about the shortage of "eligible" men available to black women for establishing families. Margaret Black has recorded the thoughts, words, deeds, and feelings of black churchwomen as they struggled to give meaning and definition to their lives. At the center of this text is an African-American and female consciousness rarely seen at this early date. The story is set in the village of St. Michaels, which has a small black population and one black church that appears to be affiliated with the African Methodist Episcopal denomination (the Mite Missionary Society suggests this connection).

Margaret Black, similar to Pauline Hopkins in "Bro'r Abr'm Jimson's Wedding," centers this story in the church, emphasizing the centrality of the institution in the lives of African Americans. The story focuses as well on who will marry the most eligible bachelor. The plot revolves around the activities of the Ladies' Aid Society, which is actively engaged in preparing for the arrival of Reverend Jonathan Steele, a twenty-five-year-old minister who is single. The Society is made up primarily of the wives of the all-male board of trustees and board of stewards, some of the most powerful women in the church.

Although black churchwomen have been traditionally perceived as being subordinate and powerless in a male-dominated institution, Black creates narrative strategies which stress the power that these women wielded through their organizations. In doing so, she effectively recovers their voices and their sense of autonomy.

A Christmas Party That
Prevented a Split in the Church

Part I

"Goodness," exclaimed Milly Brown. "All these things to move and dust, they're a sight and if I had my way, I'd get rid of some of them. No single man needs all this trash around, especially a minister."

"Always getting rid of something," said Sara Simpson," I declare you are the limit; perhaps you'll want to be getting rid of your daughter Alice—now we are having a new minister and he a single man."

"I guess you are the one who'll be wanting the minister to marry them," laughed Milly. But Sara Simpson did not see the joke, you see Sara was past thirty—and did not like it mentioned—had a lovely home in town and everybody knew she was sore at Mrs. Jake Todd because Jake preferred her when she was Margaret Clayton instead of Sara Simpson—whose father was the leading lawyer in town and who gave his wife and daughter anything they wanted.

Sara was a pretty girl, but Margaret was much prettier and had such a sweet disposition that everybody loved her, even if she did have to wear cheap cotton dresses—and her hats and coats two winters and couldn't afford furs. But Sara snubbed poor Margaret every chance she got and poor Milly Brown also—because she was Margaret's friend.

Mrs. Milly Brown was a widow with only one daughter who lived beyond the town a lonely way and made her living by doing plain sewing.

You see there was only one church in the very small town—you or I would call it a village—which would surely have insulted the small population of St. Michaels because they felt themselves very important people and more especially now—as they were able to support a minister by themselves.

No more circuit riding minister for them. Since attaining the dignity of supporting a minister and having a parsonage rent free—they had organized a Mite Society for the grown people and a Helping Hand Society for the young folks and a Sunday Afternoon Literary Society, hence the self-satisfied feeling among them.

Their last pastor had been a married man with a large family, a wife and six children, and the poor man had so much trouble and such poor charges (which is the fate of a good many Methodist ministers) that he felt after he got to St. Michaels that he should take a rest, and he rested so well, and so long, that the people sent the Bishop word they did not want him back. So the good Bishop had now sent them not only a young man, but a single one, and St. Michaels folks were going out of their way to make things pleasant for the new minister.

He was very young and considered a genius, and as St. Michaels always gave the parsonage ready furnished and found the good parson coal and wood—they felt that since this was a young man they should go a step further and stock his pantry with all things needful and have him a good housekeeper, so they had installed old Aunt Eliza West as his housekeeper.

There had been a meeting of the Ladies' Aid Society, and a Committee for the pastor's arrival.

The Board of Trustees and Board of Stewards had also held meetings, but the Ladies' Aid had taken things in their hands and the men were well content to step aside and let them do the work—as most of their wives belonged to the Aid Society and those whose wives did not, thought it good policy to not object.

So there was just lots of help—because as Mrs. Orion Tucker remarked, "Wherever they had a married minister all the women stayed at home except a few old stand-bys who could always be depended on, but if he was a single man, every spinster and young girl and married woman in the town was in evidence to help, they had all they needed and more."

So they scrubbed floors—cleaned paints and windows—and swept and dusted and polished dishes and silver until it seemed as tho the things would surely come to life and cry out—enough! oh, enough! or melt into nothing.

At last everything was in readiness and St. Michaels was in a state of expectancy.

Only Brother Tucker and Sister Marion Ford had attended the conference at Greenville and neither of them could give a very clear account of what he looked like.

Brother Tucker said, "He was a pretty pert and spry looking youngster," and Sister Marion Ford said, "He was a handsome young chap—straight and tall as a young poplar and with the snappiest black eyes she'd ever seen—altogether quite 'stinguished looking."

"But," as Marie Phillips sarcastically remarked, "you can't depend on either one of these old folks, because everybody is 'pert' and spry to Brother Tucker, who walks and talks pretty slick and as for Sister Marion Ford—Oh pshaw! she can't see good anyway."

But "all's well that ends well"—and Rev. Jonathan Steele had arrived and was quite all both Brother Tucker and Sister Ford had described, and more, some of them thought. In plain words—"he came, he saw, he conquered" and after several months with the town folks—he was still "the new preacher"—at least he was as new as seven months steady wear in a small town could leave him. You see new silver does not tarnish very quickly and Rev. Steele was still untarnished. Of course he made mistakes—and this Thursday night at the meeting of the Ladies'

Aid they were discussing the fact that the Rev. Mr. Steele did not or could not seem to grasp the fact that Mrs. John Taylor was the leader of the Ladies' Aid and a shining light in the church, and that Mrs. Orion Tucker was to be church treasurer for life and that the Trustees and Stewards' Boards were composed of life time members and also that Mrs. St. Anthony was the head deaconess of the church and as her husband had donated the ground on which the church stood and donated five thousand dollars towards the building fund, she must be consulted on all matters pertaining to the welfare of the church.

How was the Rev. Jonathan Steele, not a day over twenty-five and a young snip just out of college, as Mrs. Tucker emphatically declared, to realize the importance of each separate man's and woman's work in his ever increasing congregation.

Although after seven months—if he really had failed to grasp these many cited facts—it was no fault of the members of St. Michaels' Church.

"Things seem to be moving along rather smoothly," remarked Mrs. Phillips—"I think the Reverend has commenced to appreciate his charge"—which remark was due to the fact that the Rev. Steele had lately congratulated Mrs. Phillips on her executive ability.

The ladies were lingering over the task of sorting out table linen and dishes after the yearly oyster supper for the benefit of the Stewards' Board.

"Yes," said Mrs. Phillips, "how our girls did work; they are coming into the church and working like soldiers, and are not near so thoughtless and silly as they used to be."

"Oh yes!" said Mrs. Tucker sarcastically. "It is really remarkable how they work. An unmarried minister can inspire so much enthusiasm among spinsters—and women with marriageable daughters."

"Well, I'm not making any unkind remarks," said Mrs. Phillips virtuously.

"Well," replied Mrs. Tucker—"neither am I, but I can't help noticing things when they happen right under your nose. I have eyes to see with and although we might not care to spread it broad cast, we can all see the difference between the treatment accorded Rev. Butler and that given Rev. Steele. You see Rev. Butler was an antiquated married man, while Rev. Steele is a very live young man. With Rev. Butler we crawled along and the community hardly knew we existed, while now we are increasing by leaps and bounds—fairly flying."

"Well," said Mrs. Phillips, "it's natural isn't it. The young—"

"Of course it's natural," broke in Mrs. Tucker. "Life is just a succession of thrills anyway, and we all run after that we don't have. Didn't I run a little after my old man Orion, and didn't you run after Nathan?"

"No, I didn't," snapped Mrs. Phillips, "I never took one step out of my way for Nathan Phillips."

"Oh, well, you grabbed him mighty quick when he asked you—and that's what I'm thinking about these girls and old maids—any one of them could grab Rev. Steele mighty quick if he asks them."

A light laugh startled them and made them turn rather quickly— they had forgotten they were in church.

"I'm glad my girl lives such a distance from the church—that she can't take part in everything. Until she does her school work and helps me a little, she has no time to join church clubs and Ladies' Aid Societies, and talk scandal," said the irrepressible Milly Brown. "But I guess you'll soon have a new member any way for your society— because Hannah Burke Stark has come home and is occupying the Powell place adjoining us. You remember her don't you Mrs. Phillips."

"Well, I should say," replied Mrs. Phillips, "she married young Dr. Stark of Cleveland. So she's home. Is her husband with her?"

"Oh no, she is a widow," said Milly, "and I'm thinking a pretty wealthy one at that."

"You don't say," said Mrs. Tucker. "How do you know?"

"Well, by the style of her and the way she lives and the improvements she is making in the place. She has house servants, a gardener, and chauffeur and a man to tend the farm and she has had the house all done over. You won't know the place when it is finished. And she has an immense touring car, and the dearest coupe she runs herself. Then she rides and has a beautiful thoroughbred horse and has just the finest of clothes."

"Well," said Mrs. Phillips, "that don't sound like she'll be much of a church worker—but we'll wait and see. You never can tell."

"Alice says she's lovely," replied Milly. "She's been very good to Alice."

"We must call," said Mrs. Tucker, "it is so lonely out there."

"Yes, it's lonely with only Milly and her Alice for neighbors," retorted Mrs. Phillips. "But I'll have to study over it first. You see I knew Hannah before she was married, and she was always a mighty independent little piece and held her head very high."

"Oh, that's nothing," said Mrs. Tucker, "birds fly high too, but they always come down for water. So perhaps your Hannah was lonesome and home-sick for the sight of home and old faces, the reason she returned to St. Michaels."

"Well—we'll soon see," said Mrs. Phillips. And see they did in a way that didn't suit St. Michaels folks at all.

The following Thursday the Ladies' Aid met at Mrs. St. Anthony's. They always met at Mrs. St. Anthony's whenever they could—and that was nine times out of ten—because her home was just a few steps below the parsonage and they could see Rev. Steele whenever he came out or in or had visitors, and then being close—he sometimes dropped in and took tea with the ladies, only when he came they served cocoa and tea cakes because it was more fashionable.

But this Thursday they were doomed to disappointment because Rev. Steele came out his gate—and every girl and old maid's heart beat a little faster, and each one either took her little chamois and touched up her nose a little for fear it might be shiny or patted her hair a little smoother or tucked a hair pin a little tighter—but with a gasp, of astonishment—instead of turning in at Mrs. St. Anthony's and sauntering slowly up the walk as usual—he walked briskly by without so much as a glance at the house.

The Ladies' Aiders sat as though paralyzed—and little Marie Phillips, who thought he was on the eve of proposing to her, said, "Well the nerve of him. I wonder where he can be going?"

"Well if you say so," said Lillian Tucker, "I'll run and ask him."

"Now girls," said Miss Sara Simpson, "don't get excited, you know a pastor of a church like ours has so many important duties to attend to that he can't always attend our meetings."

"Don't make excuses Sara," retorted Mrs. Phillips, "there isn't anything more important than our meetings."

"Stung," laughed Lillian Tucker—"perhaps he has gone to see the great and beautiful widow Stark"—and as though she had been a prophetess—the widow and the pastor came into view quietly talking and seemingly interested only in each other.

Everybody looked and if only the pastor could have known each one's thought of him—who watched him so closely. The young girls were mostly amused but the spinsters and married women were not so charitably inclined.

Mrs. Stark was dressed in a fashionable tailor made suit with hat, gloves, and shoes to match and carried an armful of beautiful hot-house tea roses.

At his gate they stopped and she put out her hand and took his and put all the roses in them—and then [she] stooped and buried her face in them as though loath to part with them and when she raised her face he said something to her and buried his face in them as she had done.

"Look," said Miss Sara Simpson with a look of disgust on her face—"he is kissing and caressing them because she did so—right out in the street, isn't it disgusting, and he seems to like her too and here last Sunday he took us to task about expensive clothes, and street walking and flirting and love-making in public and—"

"Do hush Sara," said Mrs. St. Anthony. "Look at the bunch of roses, it hasn't cost a cent less than $5. I imagine I can smell them here. I wonder if he really likes roses?"

Mrs. Tucker seemed genuinely amused at some unspoken thought and her quick light laugh fell jarringly upon the members.

"Oh dear!" said one, "do keep quiet."

"I don't see anything to laugh about," said another.

"Well he likes roses well enough to keep those," said some one else.

"It seems so," said another.

The gate clicked shut and Mrs. Stark walked along up the street, unconscious of the storm she had stirred up.

"If she is so intimate with him, it's a wonder she wouldn't come to church and help with the church work or join the society and help to do something, and she wouldn't have time to flirt with the minister," said Mrs. St. Anthony.

"Has anyone"—asked Mrs. Phillips—"asked Hannah Stark to join our society or one of our church clubs?"

No one had—

"I'll do it now," said Mrs. Phillips.

"Hurry or she'll be out of sight," they urged. They followed Mrs. Phillips to the door.

Mrs. Stark had gone by—but she came back with a smile on her face, and not a little amused at being accosted thus. Mrs. Phillips stood on the top step and resolved to do what she thought was her duty.

"I am Mrs. Phillips—Mrs. Stark, and remember you as Hannah Burke—we saw you talking to Rev. Steele"—she said by way of introduction—"We thought you might like to join our society or our young people's Helping Hand Club."

Mrs. Phillips was unaware how she spoke—her voice cut the air like a whip saw—and said plainly—we do not want you, but you should think it your duty,—and an honor, that I, Mrs. Lawyer Phillips, should ask you to join.

Mrs. Stark's eyes snapped—and her head went up a little higher—"Thank you"—she said—"I feel honored. Does your pastor belong to these clubs and is he a member of the Church Aid Society?"

"No," exclaimed indignant Mrs. Phillips.

"Then I'm sorry to decline the honor, but I can't possibly belong to anything of which he is not a member, and not under his direct supervision."

She was gone, and Mrs. Phillips had to be helped in the house to the couch, and Mrs. St. Anthony was so angry she was blue in the face. I thought she would explode, and poor Miss Sara Simpson fainted; in fact everybody was out of commission but Mrs. Tucker, who got on everybody's nerves by laughing and saying—

"I like that woman. She's got spunk and brains enough to give you a dose of nicely sugar-coated pills that helps immensely."

Before night all St. Michaels had heard the story of the roses and the invitation to join the club and it did not lose anything in the telling.

Unconsciously, all St. Michaels formed a detective bureau to watch the pastor.

They played detective and they watched poor Rev. Steele's every move and at last [they] had come to the conclusion that he was hopelessly in love with the widow.

Poor Mrs. Stark, did she know how St. Michaels regarded her, or what they thought of her? If she did—no one in St. Michaels was any the wiser.

Then one Sunday morning just a few weeks before Xmas, Mrs. Stark appeared at church, and the Ladies' Aid members that were present, I'm afraid paid more attention to Mrs. Stark than they did to the sermon, in fact I'm afraid they could not have given the sermon's text if asked—but I'm sure they could have told you all about Mrs. Stark's costume.

At the Thursday afternoon meeting following, Mrs. Stark was the topic as usual.

"What's wrong with her now," said Mrs. Tucker. "At first she was just a butterfly and a flirt, then she was haughty and proud, then she did not attend church, she was a heathen, now she attends church, you are still faultfinding and she is a hypocrite—what is wrong with her now?" she challenged.

"Well she is not a member," said Mrs. Phillips, "and she just came to have the pastor walk her home."

"Well whose business is it if she does? Don't you think Rev. Steele is old enough to look after himself?" said Mrs. Tucker.

"Well, what do you expect of us? You'd be suspicious yourself—after those roses—if you were not [so] in love with both her and the pastor, that it takes all your time to champion her cause and snub your neighbors, all on account of a city woman, who is supposed to have plenty of money and fine clothes. I think she's bewitched you," remarked Mrs. Phillips, "as you have gone clean daft about her."

"Well I'm satisfied," retorted Mrs. Tucker, "my opinion of the matter [is] that we will lose all the ground we've gained—and waste our profits—if we don't stop this unseasonable, unreasonable squabbling—come to our senses and adjust the differences which have suddenly sprung up between the pastor and this society all on account of his attention to a woman, and we are not sure that he is paying special attention to her. Because a man calls on a woman or walks home with her is no sign he wants to marry her."

"Quite a sermon Mrs. Tucker, have you taken the Rev. Steele's place? Who elected you his champion," sarcastically asked Mrs. St. Anthony. "Perhaps the members here are not to your liking and you wish to resign."

"I am not trying to take anyone's place," retorted Mrs. Tucker — "but three weeks from now is Xmas, and this is hold together time — not hold-up or split-up time. A similar opportunity to have a big Xmas fete in the church and to get and keep all the younger folks working may never occur again and I move we take time by the forelock and get busy.

"The pastor gave those roses to old Mother Carey," explained Mrs. Tucker triumphantly, "and I bet Mrs. Stark knew all about it — perhaps she sent them by him."

"Humph!" said Miss Sara Simpson, "Jonathan Steele is a sly one — probably his pricking conscience told him the Ladies' Aid was watching."

Part II

"The marriageable women of our church are nice and would be a plus for any man. They are as pretty and dutiful as he'll find elsewhere, but he won't marry one of them. He can't see the pot over the sill of the

  Margaret Black

window for the rain," said Mrs. Phillips. "If there was another church here we would leave, my husband says."

"And I would follow you," said Mrs. St. Anthony and Mrs. Ford in chorus—and then the trouble started.

Rev. Steele called a meeting of the Mite Society—and Ladies' Aid Society—and organized a Young People's Get-together for Wednesday evening at 7 o'clock.

Although the three organizations consisted of seventy-five or more members among them, only five young folks and three old ones turned out—Milly Brown, Mrs. Tucker and Mrs. Ford.

Rev. Steele made no comment on the presence or the absence of the members.

"Well," said he, "this will be my first meeting with you, and as you have all been faithful the past seven months, I thought with your help—we will have a Xmas this year that will leave a sweet memory to every person at St. Michaels as long as life itself.

"Are you willing to help?"

"We certainly are," exclaimed Mrs. Tucker, and the rest acquiesced.

Several committees were appointed and those who were absent were notified of their appointments and the jobs they were expected to do.

Some agreed half-heartedly and some refused point blank to not only serve on the committees, but to attend church—and a split in the church of St. Michaels loomed large on the horizon.

Sunday morning two weeks before Xmas, Rev. Steele preached his second formal sermon in St. Michaels Church on "Gossip" and truly St. Michaels was in an up-heaval.

No one knew if he was aware of the feelings of his congregation or not. He had chosen "Gossip" for his subject, but in the middle of his sermon he told his congregation that no matter what happened—even if he was to render his resignation within the next twelve hours—he would have the satisfaction of knowing that he had been a p-a-s-t-o-r and not a figure head.

He got everyone to thinking and Mrs. St. Anthony wondered if "he could rightly know what had been said about him by the Ladies' Aid."

"It makes no difference if he does," said Mrs. Phillips. "It would do him not to know what I think of him."

"Humph," said Mrs. Tucker, "much he cares for your opinion or any one of the rest of us, I'm thinking. He believed Rev. Butler to be led by the nose wheresoever a set of crazy men and women chose to lead him."

When Frank Coombs resigned as superintendent of the Sunday School, they thought he'd be coaxed to remain, but when no one coaxed, only a few old heads—and Harry Young was asked to fill his place—it was like stirring up a hornet's nest. "Mrs. Coombs and her sister, Mrs. Cook, do come to church—but I declare they would be better at home," said Mrs. Ford.

  Margaret Black

"Mrs. Cook told me," said Mrs. Phillips, "she looked at the pipes of the organ so long and so hard that she could tell every move on them and where, with her eyes shut, and it was no wonder they had not fallen down on her before this.

"Old Mrs. Lake sits with the book up-side down—and pretends to read, when we all know she can't tell A from B if they were a yard high. Even the members of the Trustees' and Stewards' Boards are at logger heads, because he appointed some young men, who have lately joined the church, on the boards and asked for the resignation of some of the old men on the board. They had been on the board so long they were moss-covered."

"Well I can't see," said Mrs. St. Anthony, "why he wanted to change things around."

"I can tell you," said Mrs. Tucker, "he thinks if you want to keep young people in the church after they join—you should put them to work and make them feel they are wanted. You see it's useless to try to hold young folks anywhere now-a-days unless they have something to do. There is too much of this wanting to be boss all the time and a few old fogies wanting the church to stay in a rut and keeping things like they were fifty years ago. Times are changing and you've simply got to change with them or get out of the running. A piece of antique china is admired for its age—but it is put upon the shelf for safe keeping and admired for what it was and is not for its present use. So it is with us, we must either help the younger folks along or stand to be put on the shelf. I say live and let live.

"The whole thing in a nut-shell is he hasn't paid the attention to our marriageable daughters we thought he should," said Mrs. Tucker. "He goes among us—loves us—and thinks for our interest—which should make him loved by all—but it seems there must always be a few discontented ones among the flock."

"What's the use of jangling," said Mrs. Todd. "Let us get busy. What will you give towards the Christmas fete, Mrs. Hunter?"

"I—oh, don't know," said Mrs. Hunter—"I guess 2 quarts of cream and a chocolate cake."

"What will you give, Mrs. Phillips?"

"Not one single thing," she replied, "count me out of it. Mr. Phillips says we'll not take part in the affair."

"What will you give Mrs. Tucker."

"A cake, a chicken, 2 lbs of coffee and help to do whatever I can."

"And you Mrs. Ford?"

"Oh—Mr. Ford says we'll not take any part in it."

"Look here ladies, before I go any further," said Mrs. Todd, "let me ask you that won't help, please do not hinder."

"Goodness gracious—Margery Todd put that list up—and don't use the Ladies' Aid's time for such foolishness," said Mrs. Phillips.

"Alright," said Mrs. Todd, "but I'll call on every one of you tomorrow."

  Margaret Black

"I can't get over that sermon," said Mrs. St. Anthony—hopping back to the old subject.

"Neither can I," said Mrs. Phillips.

"There goes the Reverend and the widow now!" said Marie Phillips.

"Well that caps the climax," said old Mrs. Ford bitterly, as the Reverend and the widow passed out of sight.

But she was mistaken. Something happened a few days later that threw the community into a tizzy. The whole community began to talk to each other through back doors, across to their neighbors, or talked across fences—back and front by the hour. They even called special meetings to discuss it, in fact everybody you met was talking about it and everybody held a squared white envelope which contained a beautifully printed square white card which was drawn out and compared with other cards just like it, and soon St. Michaels awoke to the fact that every member and non-member of St. Michaels, men, women and young people—was invited to an elaborate Christmas party.

In the words of Mrs. Tucker—"Mrs. Stark was giving a big Christmas blow out."

After the first surprise was over, everybody was wondering why he or she had been invited and one and all came to the conclusion, to get in with St. Michaels' folks—except the Ladies' Aid—who said Mrs. Stark was taking this way to show she was sorry for the way she had acted.

Though, Mrs. Tucker says—"What she had to be sorry for was beyond her."

Then came the getting ready for the party. The boy that blew the mouth organ thought his checkered pants and blue coat with his new tan shoes was just the thing. The sexton's wife bought a pretty white dimity dress—much too tight and which seemed to make her look twice as broad. But the leaders of the church—the Ladies' Aid—such a flurry—such a bustling.

Of course Mrs. St. Anthony, Mrs. Phillips—the lawyer's wife, and the doctor's wife, Mrs. Jameson—and Miss Simpson and Mrs. White, and their daughters could and did go to the city to get their outfit, and as Marie Phillips told Mrs. Tucker the dresses will be real creations of art.

But the rest of St. Michaels had to be content to buy in St. Michaels, and to trust to Milly Brown, Violet Cunningham, and old Mrs. Thomas to make them.

Said Mrs. Tucker—"I'm mighty glad I'm invited—and I'm satisfied with any old plum-colored silk, because it's no use to go to that party trying to out dress Mrs. Stark, because she knows how to dress, and as Mr. Tucker says, she could put on my old plum-colored silk and look like an angel in it, with that mop of hair as black as a raven's wing and eyes as black as coal and a complexion like a rose leaf—she looks like a big doll anyway. I'll dress to suit Mrs. Tucker who is short and

  Margaret Black

inclined to stoutness and past forty-five and not like Hannah," with which common sense remarks.

Mrs. Tucker took her ancient plum-colored silk and sewed some real lace in the sleeves and fixed a dainty white fichu around the neck which would tend to make her look decidedly sweet and motherly and altogether lovely.

The wonderful night rolled around all too quickly, they went in conveyances of all kinds—wagons, ancient carriages, buggies, daytons, and autos, all carried their quota of guests.

But Mrs. Tucker and Mrs. Todd said the street cars were good enough for them, so accompanied by Mr. Tucker and Mr. Todd, they wended their way there.

Everybody went—not one invitation was refused or ignored—they were there to eat, to listen, to enjoy, and above all to see how Rev. Steele and Mrs. Stark would act before the people of St. Michaels.

When they arrived, they were more than surprised at the display that met their gaze, and they were awed into silence—and as they gazed, they, one and all, thought how beautiful.

Even Mrs. St. Anthony and Mrs. Phillips and Miss Simpson who were used to such things, had never seen anything quite as elaborate as this. Whatever else they may think, there was only one thing that could be said of her in regards to this Christmas party—it was gotten together on an elaborate scale and it was well done.

When they entered, they were turned over to the maid who took them up stairs and ushered them into a room, where wraps were removed and checked and they had a chance to pin back a stray strand of hair or adjust a ribbon if they so wished, then when returning down stairs were announced by the butler—who was none other than young Bill Winston, hired and dressed up for the occasion, and who walked so straight and held his head so high that they wondered if he could see the folks he announced.—They entered timidly and in nervous little groups, following each other sheep-fashion, to the place where the hostess stood to receive them—not knowing, the most of them, whether to shake hands or simply bow, nor what to do with themselves afterwards.

But once the hostess greeted them they forgot their self-consciousness and their nervousness in looking at the vision of loveliness that had greeted them. She wore a lovely dress—"a most wonderful gown," Mrs. Tucker said, "of some sort of white stuff—that looked soft, billowy clouds of fleece—dotted here and there with stones that shone like hundreds of stars and sparkled like thousands of diamonds under the blazing electric light"; and as old Mrs. Ford said, "she made everybody feel so homey and comfortable."

"Well I declare," said Mrs. Phillips, "a bridal costume as I live"—as she gazed at the little spray of orange blossoms that nestled so lovingly in Mrs. Stark's abundant dark hair.

  Margaret Black

"Do you know," said Sara Simpson. "I believe she has invited us all to her wedding."

Some one whispered, "Isn't she glorious?" And it floated from one to the other around the room, there was a gentle hum as of bees in the distance, everybody seemed happy.

"I wonder where the Reverend is?" said old Mrs. St. Anthony.

Time passed and the older folks commenced to get restless—the younger ones were in dream-land and as the orchestra music was wafted so softly and temptingly on the air the younger folks looked longingly at the waxed floor glistening in the distance and wished the pastor would not show up so they could dance.

"Oh!" said Marie Phillips, "just for one turn on that floor"—and the rest echoed her wish.

People commenced to move nervously about, and to stand and talk in excited little groups. There was a hint of something in the air that no one could tell what it was—where was Rev. Steele? Why didn't the wedding take place? Who was going to marry them?

Even Mrs. Stark was getting restless, her cheeks were flushed, and her eyes fairly glistened and kept roaming toward the side entrance. Her hands played nervously with her fan—the young folks were almost tempted to ask could they dance.

The time seemed to pass so slowly and a wave of restlessness hard to control was fast gaining possession of the guests.

Everybody took to cautiously watching Mrs. Stark, who was walking aimlessly here and there around the rooms and talking nervously to first one guest and then another, but it was noticed that her glance wandered continually toward the side entrance, the music itself seemed to accelerate the restlessness of the crowd.

Suddenly the music changed—as the strains of Lohengrin's Wedding March pealed joyously forth—the side door was thrown wide and the footman announced in a stentorian voice—"Mr. and Mrs. Jonathan Steele."

Everybody turned to look, and there standing framed in the doorway, smilingly stood the Rev. Jonathan Steele, and standing by his side—clinging to his arm stood his bride—timid little Alice Brown, in a simple white dress, looking for all the world like a happy Brown Thrush.

Of course everybody in the room could have told you, that they knew it was Alice Brown the pastor had been coming out into the lonely end of town to see.

And all the girls and spinsters who had held high hopes of becoming the pastor's wife, will tell you that Rev. Steele is a passably good-looking man, but he is a long way from being a handsome one.

"Sour grapes," says Mrs. Tucker. But the Ladies' Aid and the Helping Hand ladies just looked at Alice's mother Milly Brown, and wondered to themselves how she ever kept it to herself.

But it did not matter, only to a few like Miss Sara Simpson—whose chances of [finding a] husband were getting fewer each year and to Mrs. Phillips—who was anxious to see Marie safely settled, and to Mrs. St. Anthony, who could not now meddle so easily in the pastor's household affairs. To the majority, he had married a St. Michaels girl and that was the main thing, so the church was decorated, good things donated, and the Christmas fete was a royal reception to the pastor and his bride. And to this day St. Michaels' folks love to tell of the Christmas party and how it prevented a split in the church.

After Many Days: A Christmas Story

FANNIE BARRIER WILLIAMS

Fannie Barrier Williams

Fannie Barrier Williams devoted her life to eradicating racism and gender discrimination against black women. Born in Brockport, New York, she was the youngest of three children of Anthony J. and Harriet Prince Barrier. Born free, she represented the third generation of a family of free blacks who had enjoyed cordial relations with whites in Brockport. She attended the integrated local public schools and graduated from the academic and classical course of the State Normal School at Brockport in 1870. During the 1870s and 1880s, she taught school in the South and in Washington, D.C., and studied at the New England Conservatory of Music in Boston and the School of Fine Arts in Washington. In 1887, she married S. Laing Williams of Georgia, a graduate of the University of Michigan and an honors graduate of the Columbian Law School in Washington (later named the George Washington University Law School). From 1893 to 1920, she was highly celebrated as a journalist, lecturer, and clubwoman.

It was in the South during the 1870s that Fannie Barrier's innocence concerning racism was destroyed. Having moved and socialized freely with whites in Brockport, she had felt on equal terms with them. In the South she had a rude awakening, discovering that social justice was a right extended only to whites. She bristled at southern Jim Crow laws and the strict racial segregationist codes and rejected the notion that because of her Negro blood, she belonged to an inferior race.

Fannie Barrier Williams gained national recognition in May 1893 in Chicago when she addressed the departmental congress of the National Association of Loyal Women of American Liberty at the World's Congress of Representative Women. Speaking on "The Intellectual Progress and Present Status of the Colored Women of the United States Since the Emancipation Proclamation," she stated that black women "are the only women in the country for whom real ability, virtue, and special talents count for nothing when they become applicants for respectable employment." Months later in an address to the World's Parliament of Religions she stated that "it should be the province of religion to unite, and not separate, men and women according to superficial differences of race lines." Extensive press coverage brought her notoriety and a deluge of speaking engagements.

Williams's 1894 nomination and later controversial admission to the elite white Chicago Women's Club created great dissension in the General Federation of Women's Clubs, as some white women withdrew their memberships and others threatened to do so. Her membership forced the organization to confront its exclusionary policies.

Williams was a staunch supporter of the militant protest tradition of Frederick Douglass. However, after 1900, she joined her husband in actively espousing the Booker T. Washington accommodationist ideology. It is likely that this change was related to her husband's need for Washington's support for a federal position, which he received in 1908 with an appointment to the post of federal assistant district attorney in Chicago.

As a writer, Williams was primarily a journalist. However, in 1902, she wrote "After Many Days: A Christmas Story," which appears to be partly autobiographical. Reflecting on miscegenation and its impact upon the lives of black women, particularly women whose lives were tied up with those of their white masters, it is likely that she included details of her mulatto family's history. Fannie, like Gladys Winne, the heroine, was very fair with straight hair and Caucasian features.

"After Many Days," set in the mid-1880s in Virginia, is principally about the fate of Gladys Winne, the daughter of a slave mother and white father. Raised as a white woman, a few days before Christmas she discovers that Aunt Linda, a former slave on the Edwards plantation, is her grandmother.

Published in 1902, this short story uses social criticism to explore issues regarding the legacy of slavery. One of the questions raised by this story is Who is black? In the nineteenth and early twentieth centuries, most states defined in law the meaning of "Negro." Depending upon the number of white antecedents, one could be defined as an "octoroon" or "quadroon." In most cases if one had one-thirty-second of Negro blood, one was defined as black. It did not matter if a person's skin was pale white, eyes were blue, and there were no distinguishable Negroid features. Introducing this issue, the story states, "Aunt Linda had felt and known the horrors of slavery, but could she have known that after twenty years of freedom, nothing in the whole range of social disgrace could work such terrible disinheritance to man or woman as the presence of Negro blood, seen or unseen, she would have given almost life itself rather than to have condemned this darling of her love and prayers to so dire a fate."

Given that so much has been published about the "tragic mulatto" and how black women are used for sex but rarely treated with love, it is important to discuss Williams's treatment of this issue. This is particularly true because this story focuses upon the plight of Gladys Winne and unlike her counterparts, she does not end up being the tragic mulatto. More importantly, Williams, as a social and political activist, constantly spoke and wrote about how slavery almost destroyed black womanhood. Although Gladys Winne is the result of an interracial liaison, she is not destroyed by it, primarily because her white father protected her from knowledge of her background.

Using Aunt Linda as narrator, Williams reflects upon the plight of black girls, particularly beautiful mulattos, who are viewed as sex objects. Aunt Linda speaks about how she shielded Alice from the advances of lecherous white males who devalued black womanhood. Relating the reaction of her master when he discovers that his son wants to marry Alice, she emphasizes the taboos against marrying a black woman, even one who is indistinguishable from other white people.

Following the lead of Frances Ellen Watkins Harper (in *Iola Leroy: Or Shadows Uplifted,* 1892), Fannie Barrier Williams emphasizes the "horror of slavery" as visited upon the most effective heroine of the antebellum abolitionist novel, the beautiful refined mulatto. Like Iola Leroy, Gladys Winne is educated and is the offspring of a legal marriage between the son of a wealthy plantation owner and a slave. Winne is raised as an upper-class white woman with privileges shared by few white women of her time. When she discovers that she is black, she worries whether Paul will continue to love her and want to marry her.

After Many Days:
A Christmas Story

Christmas on the Edwards plantation, as it was still called, was a great event to old and young, master and slave comprising the Edwards household. Although freedom had long ago been declared, many of the older slaves could not be induced to leave the plantation, chiefly because the Edwards family had been able to maintain their appearance of opulence through the vicissitudes of war, and the subsequent disasters, which had impoverished so many of their neighbors. It is one of the peculiar characteristics of the American Negro, that he is never to be found in large numbers in any community where the white people are as poor as himself. It is, therefore, not surprising that the Edwards plantation had no difficulty in retaining nearly all of their former slaves as servants under the new regime.

The stately Edwards mansion, with its massive pillars, and spreading porticoes, gleaming white in its setting of noble pines and cedars, is still the pride of a certain section of old Virginia.

One balmy afternoon a few days before the great Christmas festival, Doris Edwards, the youngest granddaughter of this historic southern home, was hastening along a well-trodden path leading down to an old white-washed cabin, one of the picturesque survivals of plantation life before the war. The pathway was bordered on either side with old-fashioned flowers, some of them still lifting a belated blossom, caught in the lingering balm of Autumn, while faded stalks of hollyhock and sunflower, like silent sentinels, guarded the door of this humble cabin.

Through the open vine-latticed window, Doris sniffed with keen delight the mingled odor of pies, cakes and various other dainties temptingly spread out on the snowy kitchen table waiting to be con-veyed to the "big house" to contribute to the coming Christmas cheer.

Peering into the gloomy cabin, Doris discovered old Aunt Linda, with whom she had always been a great favorite, sitting in a low chair before the old brick oven, her apron thrown over her head, swaying back and forth to the doleful measure of a familiar plantation melody, to which the words "Lambs of the Upper Fold," were being para-phrased in a most ludicrous way. As far back as Doris could remember, it had been an unwritten law on the plantation that when Aunt Linda's "blues chile" reached the "Lambs of the Upper Fold" stage, she was in a mood not to be trifled with. Aunt Linda had lived on the plantation so long she had become quite a privileged character. It had never been known just how she had learned to read and write, but this fact had made her a kind of a leader among the other servants, and had earned for herself greater respect even from the Edwards family. Having been a house servant for many years, her language was also better than the other servants, and her spirits were very low indeed, when she lapsed into the language of the "quarters." There was also a tradition in the family that Aunt Linda's coming to the plantation had from the first been shrouded in mystery. In appearance she was a tall yellow woman, straight as an Indian, with piercing black eyes, and bearing herself with a certain dignity of manner, unusual in a slave. Visitors to the Edwards place would at once single her out from among the other servants, sometimes asking some very uncomfortable questions concerning her. Doris, however, was the one member of the household who refused to take Aunt Linda's moods seriously, so taking in the situation at a glance, she determined to put an end to this "mood" at least. Stealing softly upon the old woman, she drew the apron from her head, exclaiming, "O, Aunt Linda, just leave your 'lambs' alone for to-day, won't you? why this is Christmas time, and I have left all kinds of nice things going on up at the house to bring you the latest news, and now, but what is the matter anyway?" The old woman slowly raised her head, saying, "I might of knowd it was you, you certainly is gettin' might sassy, chile, chile, how you did fright me sure. My min was way back in ole Carlina, jest befoh another Christmas, when de Lord done lay one hand on my pore heart, and wid de other press down de white lids over de blue eyes of my sweet Alice, O' my chile, can I evah ferget dat day?" Doris, fearing another outburst, interrupted the moans of the old woman by playfully placing her hand over her mouth, saying: "Wait a minute, auntie, I want to tell you something. There are so many delightful people up to the house, but I want to tell you about two of them especially. Sister May has just come and has brought with her [a] friend, Pauline Sommers, who sings beautifully, and she is going to sing our Christmas carol for us on Christmas eve. With them is the loveliest girl I ever saw, her name is Gladys Winne. I wish I could describe her, but I can't. I can only remember her violet eyes; think of it, auntie, not blue, but violet, just like the pansies in your garden last summer." At the mention of the last name, Aunt Linda rose, leaning on the table for support. It seemed to her as if some cruel hand had reached out of a pitiless past and clutched her heart. Doris gazed in startled awe at the storm of anguish that seemed to sweep across the old woman's face, exclaiming, "Why, auntie, are you sick?" In a hoarse voice, she answered: "Yes, chile, yes, I's sick." This poor old slave woman's life was rimmed by just two events, a birth and a death, and even these memories were hers, and not hers, yet the mention of a single name has for a moment blotted out all the intervening years and in another lowly cabin, the name of 'Gladys' is whispered by dying lips to breaking hearts. Aunt Linda gave a swift glance at the startled Doris, while making a desperate effort to recall her wandering thoughts, lest unwittingly she betray her loved ones to this little chatterer. Forcing a ghastly smile, she said, as if to herself, "As if there was only one Gladys in all dis worl, yes and heaps of Winnes, too, I reckon. Go on chile, go on, ole Aunt Linda is sure getting ole and silly." Doris left the cabin bristling with curiosity, but fortunately for Aunt Linda, she would not allow it to worry her pretty head very long.

The lovely Gladys Winne, as she was generally called, was indeed the most winsome and charming of all the guests that composed the Christmas party in the Edwards mansion. Slightly above medium height, with a beautifully rounded form, delicately poised head crowned with rippling chestnut hair, curling in soft tendrils about neck and brow, a complexion of dazzling fairness with the tint of the rose in her cheeks, and the whole face lighted by deeply glowing violet eyes. Thus liberally endowed by nature, there was further added the charm of a fine education, the advantage of foreign travel, contact with brilliant minds, and a social prestige through her foster parents, that fitted her for the most exclusive social life.

She had recently been betrothed to Paul Westlake, a handsome, wealthy and gifted young lawyer of New York. He had been among the latest arrivals, and Gladys' happiness glowed in her expressive eyes, and fairly scintillated from every curve of her exquisite form. Beautifully gowned in delicate blue of soft and clinging texture, draped with creamy lace, she was indeed as rare a picture of radiant youth and beauty as one could wish to see.

But, strange to say, Gladys' happiness was not without alloy. She has one real or fancied annoyance, which she could not shake off, though she tried not to think about it. But as she walked with Paul, through the rambling rooms of this historic mansion, she determined to call his attention to it. They had just passed an angle near a stairway, when Gladys nervously pressed his arm, saying, "Look, Paul, do you see that tall yellow woman: she follows me everywhere, and actually haunts me like a shadow. If I turn suddenly, I can just see her gliding out of sight. Sometimes she becomes bolder, and coming closer to me, she peers into my face as if she would look me through. Really there seemed to be something uncanny about it all to me; it makes me shiver. Look, Paul, there she is now, even your presence does not daunt her." Paul, after satisfying himself that she was really serious and annoyed, ceased laughing, saying, "My darling, I cannot consistently blame any one for looking at you. It may be due to an inborn curiosity; she probably is attracted by other lovely things in the same way, only you may not have noticed it." "Nonsense," said Gladys, blushing, "that is a very sweet explanation, but it doesn't explain in this case. It annoys me so much that I think I must speak to Mrs. Edwards about it." Here Paul quickly interrupted. "No, my dear, I would not do that; she is evidently a privileged servant, judging from the rightaway she seems to have all over the house. Mrs. Edwards is very kind and gracious to us, yet she might resent any criticism of her servants. Try to dismiss it from your mind, my love. I have always heard that these old 'mammies' are very superstitious, and she may fancy that she has seen you in some vision or dream, but it ought not to cause you any concern at all. Just fix your mind on something pleasant, on me, for instance." Thus lovingly rebuked and comforted, Gladys did succeed in forgetting for a time her silent watcher. But the thing that annoyed her almost more than anything else was the fact that she had a sense of being irresistibly drawn towards this old servant, by a chord of sympathy and interest, for which she could not in any way account.

But the fatal curiosity of her sex, despite the advice of Paul, whom she so loved and trusted, finally wrought her own undoing. The next afternoon, at a time when she was sure she would not be missed, Gladys stole down to Aunt Linda's cabin determined to probe this mystery for herself. Finding the cabin door ajar, she slipped lightly into the room.

Aunt Linda was so absorbed by what she was doing that she heard no sound. Gladys paused upon the threshold of the cabin, fascinated by the old woman's strange occupation. She was bending over the contents of an old hair chest, tenderly shaking out one little garment after another of a baby's wardrobe, filling the room with the pungent odor of camphor and lavender.

The tears were falling and she would hold the little garments to her bosom, crooning some quaint cradle song, tenderly murmuring, "O, my lam, my poor lil' lam," and then, as if speaking to some one unseen, she would say: "No, my darlin, no, your ole mother will shorely nevah break her promise to young master, but O, if you could only see how lovely your little Gladys has growed to be! Sweet innocent Gladys, and her pore ole granma must not speak to or tech her, mus not tell her how her own ma loved her and dat dese ole hans was de fust to hold her, and mine de fust kiss she ever knew; but O, my darlin, I will nevah tray you, she shall nevah know." Then the old woman's sobs would break out afresh, as she frantically clasped the tiny garments, yellow with age, but dainty enough for a princess, to her aching heart.

For a moment, Gladys, fresh and sweet as a flower, felt only the tender sympathy of a casual observer, for what possible connection could there be between her and this old colored woman in her sordid surroundings. Unconsciously she drew her skirts about her in scorn of the bare suggestion, but the next moment found her transfixed with the horror, a sense of approaching doom enveloping her as in a mist. Clutching at her throat, and with dilated unseeing eyes, she groped her way toward the old woman, violently shaking her, while in a terror-stricken voice she cried, "O Aunt Linda, what is it?" With a cry like the last despairing groan of a wounded animal, Aunt Linda dropped upon her knees, scattering a shower of filmy lace and dainty flannels about her. Through every fibre of her being, Gladys felt the absurdity of her fears, yet in spite of herself, the words welled up from her heart to her lips, "O Aunt Linda, what is it, what have I to do with your dead?" With an hysterical laugh, she added, "do I look like someone you have loved and lost in other days?" Then the simple-hearted old woman, deceived by the kindly note in Gladys' voice, and not seeing the unspeakable horror growing in her eyes, stretched out imploring hands as to a little child, the tears streaming from her eyes, saying, "O, Gladys," not Miss Gladys now, as the stricken girl quickly notes, "you is my own sweet Alice's little chile, O, honey I's your own dear gran-ma. You's beautiful, Gladys, but not more so den you own sweet ma, who loved you so."

The old woman was so happy to be relieved of the secret burden she had borne for so many years, that she had almost forgotten Gladys' presence, until she saw her lost darling fainting before her very eyes. Quickly she caught her in her arms, tenderly pillowing her head upon her ample bosom, where as a little babe she had so often lain.

For several minutes the gloomy cabin was wrapped in solemn silence. Finally Gladys raised her head, and turning toward Aunt Linda her face, from which every trace of youth and happiness had fled, in a hoarse and almost breathless whisper, said: "If you are my own grandmother, who then was my father?" Before this searching question these two widely contrasted types of southern conditions, stood dumb and helpless. The shadow of the departed crime of slavery still remained to haunt the generations of freedom.

Though Aunt Linda had known for many years that she was free, the generous kindness of the Edwards family had made the Emancipation Proclamation almost meaningless to her.

When she now realized that the fatal admission, which had brought such gladness to her heart, had only deepened the horror in Gladys' heart, a new light broke upon her darkened mind. Carefully placing

Gladys in a chair, the old woman raised herself like some bronze goddess of liberty. For the first time and for one brief moment she felt the inspiring thrill and meaning of the term freedom. Ignorant of almost everything as compared with the knowledge and experience of the stricken girl before her, yet a revelation of the sacred relationships of parenthood, childhood and home, the common heritage of all humanity swept aside all differences of complexion or position.

For one moment, despite her lowly surroundings and dusky skin, an equality of blood, nay superiority of blood, tingled in old Aunt Linda's veins, straightened her body, and flashed in her eye. But the crushing process of over two centuries could not sustain in her more than a moment of asserted womanhood. Slowly she lowered her arm, and, with bending body, she was again but an old slave woman with haunting memories and a bleeding heart. Then with tears and broken words, she poured out the whole pitiful story to the sobbing Gladys.

"It was this way, honey, it all happened jus before the wah, way down in ole Carolina. My lil Alice, my one chile had growed up to be so beautiful. Even when she was a tiny lil chile, I used to look at her and wonder how de good Lord evah 'lowed her to slip over my door sill, but nevah min dat chile, dat is not you alls concern. When she was near 'bout seventeen years ole, she was dat pretty that the white folks was always askin' of me if she was my own chile, the ide, as if her own ma, but den that was all right for dem, it was jest case she was so white, I knowd.

  Fannie Barrier Williams

"Tho' I lived wid my lil Alice in de cabin, I was de house maid in de 'big house,' but I'd nevah let Alice be up thar wid me when there was company, case, well I jest had to be keerful, nevah mind why. But one day, young Master Harry Winne was home from school, and they was a celebratin', an' I was in a hurry; so I set Alice to bringin' some roses fron de garden to trim de table, and there young master saw her, an' came after me to know who she was; he say he thought he knowed all his ma's company, den I guess I was too proud, an' I up an' tells him dat she was my Alice, my own lil' gurl, an' I was right away scared dat I had tole him, but he had seen huh; dat was enough, O my pore lam!" Here the old woman paused, giving herself up for a moment to unrestrained weeping. Suddenly she dried her eyes and said: "Gladys, chile, does you know what love is?" Gladys' cheeks made eloquent response, and with one swift glance, the old woman continued, "den you knows how they loved each other. One day Master Harry went to ole Master and he say: 'Father, I know you'll be awful angered at me, but I will marry Alice or no woman'; den his father say—but nevah min' what it was, only it was enough to make young master say dat he'd nevah forgive his pa, for what he say about my lil' gurl.

"Some time after that my Alice began to droop an' pine away like; so one day I say to her: 'Alice, does you an' young master love each other?' Den she tole me as how young master had married her, and that she was afeared to tell even her ma, case they mite sen him away from her forever. When young master came again he tole me all about it; jest lak my gurl had tole me. He say he could not lib withou' her. After dat he would steal down to see her when he could, bringing huh all dese pritty laces and things, and she would sit all day and sew an' cry lak her heart would break.

"He would bribe ole Sam not to tell ole Master, saying dat he was soon goin' to take huh away where no men or laws could tech them. Well, after you was bohn, she began to fade away from me, gettin' weaker every day. Den when you was only a few months ole, O, how she worshipped you! I saw dat my pore unhappy lil gurl was goin' on dat long journey away from her pore heartbroke ma, to dat home not made with hans, den I sent for young master, your pa. O, how he begged her not to go saying dat he had a home all ready for her an you up Norf. Gently she laid you in his arms, shore de mos' beautiful chile dat evah were, wid your great big violet eyes looking up into his, tho' he could not see dem for the tears dat would fall on yo sweet face. Your ma tried to smile, reaching out her weak arms for you, she said: 'Gladys,' an' with choking sobs she made us bofe promise, she say, 'promise that she shall never know that her ma was a slave or dat she has a drop of my blood, make it all yours, Harry, nevah let her know.' We bofe promised, and that night young master tore you from my breaking heart, case it was best. After I had laid away my poor unhappy chile, I begged ole Master to sell me, so as to sen me way off to Virginia, where I could nevah trace you nor look fer you, an' I nevah have." Then the old woman threw herself upon her knees, wringing her hands and saying: "O my God, why did you let her fin me?" She had quite forgotten Gladys' presence in the extremity of her distress at having broken her vow to the dead and perhaps wrought sorrow for the living.

Throughout the entire recital, told between heart-breaking sobs and moans, Gladys sat as if carved in marble, never removing her eyes from the old woman's face. Slowly she aroused herself, allowing her dull eyes to wander about the room at the patch-work covered bed in the corner; then through the open casement, from which she could catch a glimpse of a group of young Negroes, noting their coarse features and boisterous play; then back again to the crouching, sobbing woman. With a shiver running through her entire form, she found her voice, which seemed to come from a great distance, "And I am part of all this! O, my God, how can I live; above all, how can I tell Paul, but I must and will; I will not deceive him though it [may] kill me."

At the sound of Gladys' voice Aunt Linda's faculties awoke, and she began to realize the awful possibilities of her divulged secrets. Aunt Linda had felt and known the horrors of slavery, but could she have known that after twenty years of freedom, nothing in the whole range of social disgrace could work such terrible disinheritance to man or woman as the presence of Negro blood, seen or unseen, she would have given almost life itself rather than to have condemned this darling of her love and prayers to so dire a fate.

The name of Paul, breathed by Gladys in accents of such tenderness and despair, aroused Aunt Linda to action. She implored her not to tell Paul or any one else. "No one need ever know, no one ever can or shall know," she pleaded. "How could any fin' out, honey, if you did not tell them?" Then seizing one of Gladys' little hands, pink and white and delicate as a rose leaf, and placing it beside her own old and yellow one, she cried: "Look chile, look, could any one ever fin' the same blood in dese two hans [that] done kep dis secret all dese years, and now I pass it on to you an you mus' keep it for yourself for the res' of de time, deed you mus', no one need evah know."

To her dying day Aunt Linda never forgot the despairing voice of this stricken girl, as she said: "Ah, but I know; my God, what have I done to deserve this?"

With no word of pity for the suffering old woman, she again clutched her arm, saying in a stifled whisper: "Again I ask you, who was, or is my father, and where is he?" Aunt Linda cowered before this angry goddess, though she was of her own flesh and blood, and softly said: "He is dead; died when you were about five years old. He left you heaps of money, and in the care of a childless couple, who reared you as they own; he made 'em let you keep his name, I can't see why." With the utmost contempt Gladys cried, "Gold, gold, what is gold to such a heritage as this? an ocean of gold cannot wash away this stain."

Poor Gladys never knew how she reached her room. She turned to lock the door, resolved to fight this battle out for herself; then she thought of kind Mrs. Edwards. She would never need a mother's love so much as now. Of her own mother, she dared not even think. Then, too, why had she not thought of it before, this horrible story might not be true. Aunt Linda was probably out of her mind, and Mrs. Edwards would surely know.

By a striking coincidence Mrs. Edwards had noticed Linda's manner toward her fair guest, and knowing the old woman's connection with the Winne family, she had just resolved to send for her and question her as to her suspicions, if she had any, and at least caution her as to her manner.

Hearing a light tap upon her door, she hastily opened it. She needed but one glance at Gladys' unhappy countenance to tell her that it was too late; the mischief had already been done. With a cry of pity and dismay, Mrs. Edwards opened her arms and Gladys swooned upon her breast. Tenderly she laid her down and when she had regained consciousness, she sprang up, crying, "O Mrs. Edwards, say that it is not true, that it is some horrible dream from which I shall soon awaken?" How gladly would this good woman have sacrificed almost anything to spare this lovely girl, the innocent victim of an outrageous and blighting system, but Gladys was now a woman and must be answered. "Gladys, my dear," said Mrs. Edwards, "I wish I might save you further distress, by telling you that what I fear you have heard, perhaps from Aunt Linda herself, is not true. I am afraid it is all too true. But fortunately in your case no one need know. It will be safe with us and I will see that Aunt Linda does not mention it again, she ought not to have admitted it to you."

Very gently Mrs. Edwards confirmed Aunt Linda's story, bitterly inveighing against a system which mocked at marriage vows, even allowing a man to sell his own flesh and blood for gain. She told this chaste and delicate girl how poor slave girls, many of them most beautiful in form and feature, were not allowed to be modest, not allowed to follow the instincts of moral rectitude, that they might be held at the mercy of their masters. Poor Gladys writhed as if under the lash. She little knew what painful reasons Mrs. Edwards had for hating the entire system of debasement to both master and slave. Her kind heart, southern born and bred as she was, yearned to give protection and home to two beautiful girls, who had been shut out from her own hearthstone, which by right of justice and honor was theirs to share also. "Tell me, Gladys," she exclaimed, "which race is the more to be despised? Forgive me, dear, for telling you these things, but my mind was stirred by very bitter memories. Though great injustice has been done, and is still being done, I say to you, my child, that from selfish interest and the peace of my household, I could not allow such a disgrace to attach to one of my most honored guests. Do you not then see, dear, the unwisdom of revealing your identity here and now? Unrevealed, we are all your friends—" the covert threat lurking in the unfinished sentence was not lost upon Gladys. She arose, making an effort to be calm, but nervously seizing Mrs. Edwards' hand, she asked: "Have I no living white relatives?" Mrs. Edwards hesitated a moment, then said: "Yes, a few, but they are very wealthy and influential, and now living in the North; so that I am very much afraid that they are not concerned as to whether you are living or not. They knew, of course, of your birth; but since the death of your father, whom they all loved very much, I have heard, though it may be only gossip, that they do not now allow your name to be mentioned."

Gladys searched Mrs. Edwards' face with a peculiarly perplexed look; then in a plainer tone of voice, said: "Mrs. Edwards, it must be that only Negroes possess natural affection. Only think of it, through all the years of my life, and though I have many near relatives, I have been cherished in memory and yearned for by only one of them, and that an old and despised colored woman. The almost infinitesimal drop of her blood in my veins is really the only drop that I can consistently be proud of." Then, springing up, an indescribable glow fairly transfiguring and illumining her face, she said: "My kind hostess, and comforting friend, I feel that I must tell Paul, but for your sake we will say nothing to the others, and if he does not advise me, yes, command me, to own and cherish that lonely old woman's love, and make happy her declining years, then he is not the man to whom I can or will entrust my love and life."

With burning cheeks, and eyes hiding the stars in their violet depths, her whole countenance glowing with a sense of pride conquered and love exalted, beautiful to see, she turned to Mrs. Edwards and tenderly kissing her, passed softly from the room.

For several moments, Mrs. Edwards stood where Gladys had left her. "Poor deluded girl," she mused. "Paul Westlake is by far one of the truest and noblest young men I have ever known, but let him beware, for there is even now coming to meet him the strongest test of his manhood principles he has ever had to face; beside it, all other perplexing problems must sink into nothingness. Will he be equal to it? We shall soon see."

Gladys, in spite of the sublime courage that had so exalted her but a moment before, felt her resolution weaken with every step. It required almost a super-human will to resist the temptation to silence, so eloquently urged upon her by Mrs. Edwards. But her resolution was not to be thus lightly set aside; it pursued her to her room, translating itself into the persistent thought, that if fate is ever to be met and conquered, the time is now; delays are dangerous.

As she was about to leave her room on her mission, impelled by an indefinable sense of farewell, she turned, with her hand upon the door, as if she would include in this backward glance all the dainty furnishings, the taste and elegance everywhere displayed, and of which she had felt so much a part. Finally her wandering gaze fell upon a fine picture of Paul Westlake upon the mantel. Instantly there flashed into her

  Fannie Barrier Williams

mind the first and only public address she had ever heard Paul make. She had quite forgotten the occasion, except that it had some relation to a so-called "Negro problem." Then out from the past came the rich tones of the beloved voice as with fervid eloquence he arraigned the American people for the wrongs and injustice that had been perpe- trated upon weak and defenseless people through centuries of their enslavement and their few years of freedom.

With much feeling he recounted the pathetic story of this unhappy people when freedom found them, trying to knit together the broken ties of family kinship and their struggles through all the odds and hates of opposition, trying to make a place for themselves in the great family of races. Gladys' awakened conscience quickens the memory of his ter- rible condemnation of a system and of the men who would willingly demoralize a whole race of women, even at the sacrifice of their own flesh and blood.

With Mrs. Edwards' words still ringing in her ears, the memory of the last few words stings her now as then, except that now she knows why she is so sensitive as to their real import.

This message brought to her from out [of] a happy past by Paul's pictured face, has given to her a light of hope and comfort beyond words. Hastily closing the door of her room, almost eagerly, and with buoyant step, she goes to seek Paul and carry out her mission.

To Paul Westlake's loving heart, Gladys Winne never appeared so full of beauty, curves and graces, her eyes glowing with confidence and love, as when he sprang eagerly forward to greet her on that eventful afternoon. Through all the subsequent years of their lives the tenderness and beauty of that afternoon together never faded from their minds. They seemed, though surrounded by the laughter of friends and festive preparations, quite alone—set apart by the intensity of their love and happiness.

When they were about to separate for the night, Gladys turned to Paul, with ominous seriousness, yet trying to assume a lightness she was far from feeling, saying: "Paul, dear, I am going to put your love to the test tomorrow, may I?" Paul's smiling indifference was surely test enough, if that were all, but she persisted, "I am quite in earnest, dear; I have a confession to make to you. I intended to tell you this afternoon, but I could not cloud this almost our last evening together for a long time perhaps, so I decided to ask you to meet me in the library tomorrow morning at ten o'clock, will you?"

"Will I?" Paul replied; "my darling, you know I will do anything you ask; but why tomorrow, and why so serious about the matter; beside, if it be anything that is to affect our future in any way, why not tell it now?" As Gladys was still silent, he added: "Dear, if you will assure me that this confession will not change your love for me in any way, I will willingly wait until tomorrow or next year; any time can you give me this assurance?" Gladys softly answered: "Yes, Paul, my love is yours now and always; that is, if you will always wish it." There was an expression upon her face he did not like, because he could not understand it, but tenderly drawing her to him, he said: "Gladys, dear, can anything matter so long as we love each other? I truly believe it cannot. But tell me this, dear, after this confession do I then hold the key to the situation?" "Yes, Paul, I believe you do; in fact I know that you will." "Ah, that is one point gained, tomorrow; then it can have no terrors for me," he lightly replied.

Gladys passed an almost sleepless night. Confident, yet fearful, she watched the dawn of the new day. Paul, on the contrary, slept peacefully and rose to greet the morn with confidence and cheer. "If I have Gladys' love," he mused, "there is nothing in heaven or earth for me to fear."

At last the dreaded hour of ten drew near: Their "Ides of March" Paul quoted with some amusement over the situation.

The first greeting over, the silence became oppressive. Paul broke it at last, saying briskly: "Now, dear, out with this confession; I am not a success at conundrums; another hour of this suspense would have been my undoing," he laughingly said.

Gladys, pale and trembling, felt all of her courage slipping from her; she knew not how to begin. Although she had rehearsed every detail of this scene again and again, she could not recall a single word she had intended to say. Finally she began with the reminder she had intended to use as a last resort: "Paul, do you remember taking me last Spring to hear your first public address; do you remember how eloquently and earnestly you pleaded the cause of the Negro?" Seeing only a growing perplexity upon his face, she cried: "O, my love, can you not see what I am trying to say? O, can you not understand? but no, no, no one could ever guess a thing so awful"; then sinking her voice almost to a whisper and with averted face, she said: "Paul, it was because you were unconsciously pleading for your own Gladys, for I am one of them."

"What nonsense is this?" exclaimed Paul, springing from his chair; "it is impossible, worse than impossible, it can not be true. It is the work of some jealous rival; surely, Gladys, you do not expect me to believe such a wild, unthinkable story as this! If any member of this household has done this thing let us leave them in this hour. I confess I do not love the South or a southerner, with my whole heart, in spite of this 'united country' nonsense; yes, I will say it, and in spite of the apparently gracious hospitality of this household."

Gladys, awed by the violence of his indignation, placed a trembling hand upon his arm, saying: "Listen, Paul, do you not remember on the very evening of your arrival here, of my calling your attention to a tall turbaned servant with the piercing eyes? Don't you remember I told you how she annoyed me by following me everywhere, and you laughed away my fears, and lovingly quieted my alarm? Now, O Paul, how can I say it, but I must, that woman, that woman, that Negress, who was once a slave, is my own grandmother." Without waiting for him to reply, she humbly but bravely poured into his ears the whole pitiful story, sparing neither father nor mother, but blaming her mother least of all. "Ah, the pity of it!"

Without a word, Paul took hold of her trembling hands and drawing her toward the window, with shaking hand, he drew aside the heavy drapery; then turning her face so that the full glory of that sunlit morning fell upon it, he looked long and searchingly into the beautiful beloved face, as if studying the minutest detail of some matchless piece of statuary. At last he found words, saying: "You, my flower, is it possible that there can be concealed in this flawless skin, these dear violet eyes, these finely chiseled features, a trace of lineage or blood, without a single characteristic to vindicate its presence? I will not believe it; it cannot be true." Then baffled by Gladys' silence, he added, "and if it be true, surely the Father of us all intended to leave no hint of shame or dishonor on this, the fairest of his creations."

Gladys felt rather than heard a deepened note of tenderness in his voice and her hopes revived. Then suddenly his calm face whitened and an expression terrible to see swept over it. Instinctively Gladys read his thought. She knew that the last unspoken thought was of the future, and because she, too, realized that the problem of heredity must be settled outside of the realm of sentiment, her breaking heart made quick resolve.

For some moments they sat in unbroken silence; then Gladys spoke: "Good bye, Paul, I see that you must wrestle with this life problem alone as I have; there is no other way. But that you may be wholly untrammelled in your judgment, I want to assure you that you are free. I love you too well to be willing to degrade your name and prospects by uniting them with a taint of blood, of which I was as innocent as yourself, until two days ago.

"May I ask you to meet me once more, and for the last time, at twelve o'clock tonight? I will then abide by your judgment as to what is best for both of us. Let us try to be ourselves today, so that our own heart-aches may not cloud the happiness of others. I said twelve o'clock because I thought we would be less apt to be missed at that hour of general rejoicing than at any other time. Good bye, dear, 'till then." Absently Paul replied: "All right, Gladys, just as you say; I will be here."

At the approach of the midnight hour Paul and Gladys slipped away to the library, which had become to them a solemn and sacred trysting place.

Gladys looked luminously beautiful on this Christmas eve. She wore a black gauze dress flecked with silver, through which her skin gleamed with dazzling fairness. Her only ornaments were sprigs of holly, their brilliant berries adding the necessary touch of color to her unusual pallor. She greeted Paul with gentle sweetness and added dignity and courage shining in her eyes.

Eagerly she scanned his countenance and sought his eyes, and then she shrank back in dismay at his set face and stern demeanor.

Suddenly the strength of her love for him and the glory and tragedy which his love had brought to her life surged through her, breaking down all reserve. "Look at me Paul," she cried in a tense whisper, "have I changed since yesterday; am I not the same Gladys you have loved so long?" In a moment their positions had changed and she had become the forceful advocate at the bar of love and justice; the love of her heart overwhelmed her voice with a torrent of words, she implored him by the sweet and sacred memories that had enkindled from the first their mutual love; by the remembered kisses, their after-glow flooding her cheeks as she spoke, and "O, my love, the happy days together," she paused, as if the very sweetness of the memory oppressed her voice to silence, and helpless and imploring she held out her hands to him.

Paul was gazing at her as if entranced, a growing tenderness filling and thrilling his soul. Gradually he became conscious of a tightening of the heart at the thought of losing her out of his life. There could be no such thing as life without Gladys, and when would she need his love, his protection, his tenderest sympathy so much as now?

The light upon Paul's transfigured countenance is reflected on Gladys' own and as he moves toward her with out-stretched arms, in the adjoining room the magnificent voice of the beautiful singer rises in the Christmas carol, mingling in singular harmony with the plaintive melody as sung by a group of dusky singers beneath the windows.

The Prodigal Daughter:
A Story of Three Christmas Eves

Augustus M. Hodges

Augustus M. Hodges

In this story Augustus Hodges speaks about the prodigal daughter. Traditionally, African-American ministers have sermonized about the prodigal son. There are many parallels that may be drawn between the two. Hodges raises the issue of the prodigal daughter to make the point about the plight of black girls who go astray, but eventually come home.

This story was written in 1904. Hodges, a longtime resident of Brooklyn, New York, was most likely familiar with the White Rose Mission, established in 1897 in Brooklyn as a home for African-American girls and women. The mission offered a social center for community women and children as well as shelter and protection to young women coming from the South in search of employment. Without money and the support of family, a number of young women were lured and sometimes forced into prostitution by unscrupulous employment agents who ostensibly recruited poor southern black girls for domestic service in the city. Recognizing the need to address the problems confronting young women who left home seeking the more glamorous and exciting life offered by the city, Hodges focused upon the prodigal daughter.

"The Prodigal Daughter: A Story of Three Christmas Eves" is the story of Sadie Hicks, a girl who is restless and unhappy with her life. Although she had never visited New York City, Sadie was dazzled by the pleasurable images painted by her cousin and was fascinated by her silk and lace clothing. The plot opens in 1901 in a small town on Long Island, New York, and unfolds through three Christmas Eves.

This story is set at the turn of the century, when there is a great deal of emphasis on wayward girls who leave the country for the bright lights of the city, where they are met with crime and vice and frequently become sexually involved with a man who brings them down. In the typical plot, the girl either contracts a venereal disease and dies or is filled with shame because she has an "illegitimate" child. This was a major issue in America at the time. It was not an African-American problem, but an American problem, since the majority of so-called fallen girls were white.

Hodges posits the idea that young women can ruin their lives by choosing to run away from their families and friends and by taking up with strangers. Using Christmas Eve as the focus of the plot, he emphasizes the importance of being with family and those who love and support you. In the African-American tradition, Christmas is a time of homecoming, a time for black family reunion. Similar to "The Christmas Reunion Down at Martinsville," Hodges emphasizes the reunion as an element of importance in black life and culture.

The Prodigal Daughter:
A Story of Three Christmas Eves

Chapter I

CHRISTMAS EVE THE FIRST

"'Twas the night before Christmas," 1901, Andrew M. Hicks was fixing the Christmas tree. Mr. Hicks was a widower, his wife had been dead seven years. He had raised his three children—two girls and a boy—until they were twenty, eighteen, and twelve, the boy being the oldest.

Sadie Hicks, the oldest daughter sat at the dining room window in a fret. "Oh! dear me, I'm going to leave this place, it's just the same as being in jail."

"What's that?" her father asked.

"Oh," she replied, "I was only talking to myself."

"Talking to yourself! If that's the case you are putting some very bad ideas and notions in to your own head. You have no reason to complain about your home or surroundings, few girls in the same walks of life have better and many have worse. You have everything reasonable that you ask for, I don't see why you are not happy and contented, you —"

"Happy and contented," interrupted the daughter, "who can be happy in this old town, among a lot of cranks, I would like to know," and she walked out of the room before her father had finished.

Andrew Hicks was one of the leading townsmen of the village [of] B—— on Long Island, eighty miles back of the great city of New York. His business (that of a carpenter and house builder) seldom allowed him to visit greater New York and his daughter Sadie had never been there, but a female cousin who visited the Hickses during the summer had told Sadie of the wonders of the great city, its joys and its pleasures until poor Sadie's head was turned. She looked at her cousin's silk and lace dresses, they called them gowns in the city, so she was told, then looked at her blue suit and pink skirt, fine enough for a queen. She felt the feeling of discontent grow until it was incurable. It had reached this point on this Christmas Eve.

Family prayers at morning and evening were a feature of the Hicks' fireside. The church bells were ringing in the gladsome Christmas when Andrew Hicks called his family together in the little parlor for the usual evening prayer. All responded but Sadie; his aged aunt who was grandmother, mother, and housekeeper to and for the family; his "wild oats," but warm hearted son and his overgrown baby daughter.

"Where is Sadie, Aunt Catharine?" Hicks asked.

  Augustus M. Hodges

"Why up in her room, I suppose. Where do you expect her to be, in New York, Brooklyn or Philadelphia?" responded the aged aunt.

"Will," the father said, "go up stairs and tell Sadie to come down to the evening prayer."

Will went and soon returned. "She's not up there, but here is a note she left for you Pop," said the boy.

Hicks opened and read:

B—— December 24, 1901.

"Dear Father:—I know you will think I am a very bad girl when you read this but the fact of the matter is that life in the country is very slow. I'll never come here again. I can't stand an old great aunt who is cranky, a father who is too strict, a brother who is too bossy and a sister who is a little fool, so good bye forever. Do not be fool enough to try to catch me, for when you read this I will be far beyond New York City."

Your Daughter,
"Sadie."

The anger of an outraged father flashed into Hicks' eyes. He at once "hitched up" and drove to the telephone station where he sent the facts to the New York City police headquarters with a description of his daughter and the request to arrest on sight upon any charge that would hold her until he could get there.

At the Christmas dinner of the Hickses there was a vacant chair.

Chapter II

THE SECOND CHRISTMAS EVE

"'Twas the night before Christmas," 1902, that Andrew M. Hicks and his wife of three months were in the dining room fixing the last Christmas tree for his youngest daughter, the last one for the family as the days of childhood were over.

The youngest daughter was helping her step-mother to dress the tree. She found in a bureau drawer a pair of wool mitts that her older sister wore in the "long, long ago." She hung them on the tree. Her father came in; he recognized the mitts. His memory went out to the Christmas eve that they were bought for his then baby daughter, he reflected. Just then a man passed the house singing "Where Is My Wandering Boy Tonight?" He exclaimed aloud: "Oh! where is my daughter?" He fell back in his chair dead to the world for the time being.

The next day at the Christmas dinner there was a vacant chair for the erring Sadie.

   Augustus M. Hodges

Chapter III

CHRISTMAS EVE THE THIRD

"'Twas the night before Christmas," 1903, the storm was the greatest seen in years, so said the oldest citizen of B——. The streets and roads were filled with snow; the night was cold and dark. There was a family reunion that Christmas Eve at the house of Andrew M. Hicks, held that night because he was to leave B—— on the morrow for Chicago on important business. Aunt Catherine, the aunt, who was in fact filling the place of a mother, grandmother and great grandmother, presided.

There was a knock at the door. Aunt Catherine answered it. She called Hicks aside and said: "Andrew, Sadie is outside with a baby in her arms."

"Let her stay there, she has brought shame and disgrace upon an honorable family; she is dead to me; don't open the door. Let her go back to where she came from."

The old lady heard not his words; she opened the door and let the prodigal daughter in the dining room by the bright grate fire.

The younger sister, tired out by the work of helping, or in fact fixing the Christmas tree, had thrown herself across the sofa and was sleeping the sleep of innocent childhood.

The prodigal daughter gave her infant to her great aunt and kneeling besides her sister, she kissed and sobbed aloud: "Oh! my poor sister, what an example I set before you. God bless you and keep you from making the mistake I have made."

She took her infant and advanced towards her father who stood stoic like with his back to the fire.

"Oh father forgive me, I know—"

"Stand back, don't come near me. You are dead in my heart, would that you were in the family plot beside your mother. I would turn you out, were it not for the poor infant in your arms."

"But father hear my story?" she pleaded.

"I will hear nothing," was his cold reply.

The young woman looked like one mad. She placed the child on the rug before her father and excitedly exclaimed: "Father, you will, you must hear me! I have returned a wiser and better girl. I know what you think. You are mistaken. My child is of honorable birth. He is named after his grand father, Andrew Martin. My husband deserted me two months ago, since then I have worked in boarding houses in Boston to keep baby and myself alive. As I left home two years ago tonight, I now return and ask to be forgiven and taken back into heart again."

The old man gave her a cold look, but said nothing.

"Do you doubt my word?" she asked.

A cold look was her answer. She pulled from her bosom an envelope:

"Here, father, is my marriage certificate, read it and see with all my faults, I did not stoop so low as to lead an immoral life."

The old man took the envelope and slowly opened it, he carefully read the certificate and was satisfied that his grandson was born in wedlock. His heart melted; the prodigal daughter was forgiven.

The next day, Christmas, was a happy one at the Hicks home. They killed the fatted goose.

Mirama's Christmas Test

T. THOMAS FORTUNE

T. Thomas Fortune

Journalist, writer, and civil rights leader, T. Thomas Fortune was born to enslaved parents in Marianna, Florida, on October 3, 1856. After the Civil War, he briefly attended schools sponsored by the Freedmen's Bureau. In 1876, he attended Howard University in Washington, D.C., but did not graduate. While in Washington, Fortune worked for the *People's Advocate,* a black newspaper. He married Carrie C. Smiley and they had five children, two of whom reached adulthood. In 1879, Fortune moved to New York, where he worked as a printer. Around 1880 he became part owner of a weekly tabloid, the *Rumor,* which in 1881 became the *Globe,* with Fortune as its editor. Following the failure of the *Globe,* he began publishing the *New York Freeman,* which in 1887 became the *New York Age.* For many years, the *Age* had a reputation as the leading black newspaper in America, primarily because of Fortune's editorials which condemned racial discrimination and demanded full equality for black citizens. Fortune's militancy drew extensive criticism from the white press.

In spite of its successful outreach and reputation, the *Age* was not a financial success. Fortune supplemented his income by writing for other publications. In the 1890s, he wrote for the *New York Sun* and the *Boston Transcript,* and sold his freelance writing to a number of newspapers. In addition to editing the *Age,* Fortune published a book, *Black and White: Land and Politics in the South* (1884), as well as articles and short stories which appeared in other black newspapers. In 1907, he sold the *Age* to Fred R. Moore.

In 1896, the *Indianapolis Freeman* published "Mirama's Christmas Test," a story which reflects the concerns of educated black women who wished to marry men of equal stature. It is set in Jason, Florida, on Christmas Eve around 1895 in the home of Mirama Young, an upper-class, educated black woman who taught school. Mirama was the daughter and only child of a prosperous builder and contractor. Her father was a former slave and a skilled carpenter, who had been allowed to hire his time before the Civil War. Like Frederick Douglass and a small number of "trusted" slaves, he had enjoyed a status between that of a slave and a free person. As a trusted slave, he moved freely, "acting as a free person," contracting his time and giving his master an agreed-upon percentage of his earnings. This experience provided him the background and knowledge necessary to establish his own business after the war.

Mirama was engaged to be married to Alexander Simpson, a mathematician and "some what of an architect," who was the principal at the school where she taught. Simpson's father shared the views of many former slaves, including Booker T. Washington, who believed that one should acquire all the education that he or she could, but that one should also have a skill. The owner of a successful carpentry business, Simpson taught his son the carpenter's trade. His wish was that Alexander would acquire a college education and become a master carpenter and builder. His death before Alexander finished his college course, and the satisfaction of his business debts, left the family with minimal funds. Alexander could have saved the business and property, but he thought that, as an educated man, carpentry was beneath him. Essentially this was the issue which divided Mirama and Alexander, and the breach that threatened to break up their engagement.

This story echoes a theme that becomes a much-debated issue in the African-American community, and one which Carter G. Woodson immortalized in *The Miseducation of the Negro* (1933). Woodson argued that college-educated blacks had become immersed in a superficial reality, embracing empty values, and that instead of becoming educated, they were miseducated. Many college-educated blacks chose jobs in the professions, whether they were suited for them or not, because this gave them status and freed them from working with their hands. It did not matter that these jobs paid less, and that they might not offer opportunity for advancement. It is through the characters of Mirama Young and Alexander Simpson that Fortune conveys his concern about blacks who reflected these beliefs.

Fortune presents the reader with a positive model of an African-American woman who has a well-defined race and gender consciousness. He characterized Mirama as an intelligent, outspoken, independent female "intensely devoted to her race and its best interests," who is not willing to settle for a man who does not share her values. This indicates that there was a cadre of educated black women who held high expectations for themselves and their race and who were not willing to compromise and accept men who did not meet their standards. At the same time, Fortune reinforces the idea of love between black women and black men, who are striving to better themselves and their race.

Mirama's Christmas Test

It was Christmas Eve, and there was but little frost in the air, but it was frosty enough to make people move along briskly, as they stirred about Jason, in the land of sunshine and flowers, of mocking birds and alligators, getting together "Christmas things" for the little ones, and for the big ones, also; for it is very true, as the poet has said: "We are but children of a larger growth." Some of the large ones are bigger children than the small ones.

This is just what Mirama Young thought, as she sat near Alexander Simpson, in the neat parlor of her own home, in the upper part of Jason, and watched the big logs in the fireplace blaze and hiss. Mirama Young was angry.

These two young people were up-to-date Afro-Americans, with positive views on most subjects and with good sized tempers with which to back them up. They both taught school. Mr. Simpson taught for a living, but had no sort of love for the work. It seemed to him more dignified to teach school than to follow the trade of a carpenter, the mastery

of which he had acquired in his youth, and for which he had real apti-
tude. His supreme ambition was to be a lawyer, with political influence, and all that. He even dreamed that some day he might be
commissioned by the President as Minister Resident and Consul General near the court of Faraway, a soft snap much sought after by ambitious men of his race.

Mirama taught school because she liked it, and because she was
intensely devoted to her race and its best interests. She had a good
home, and had graduated from a famous seminary at the head of her
class. Her father was a builder and contractor, one of the old timers
who hired his time before the war and had been hiring the time of other
people ever since. He was a practical old gentleman, and thought there
was nothing too good for Mirama, his only child.

Mirama was engaged to be married to Alexander Simpson. They had
reached an agreement on that point, but there were others necessary to
the fulfillment of their mutual pledges upon which they were still as far
apart as the North and the South. They were argumentative and dog-
matic, were Mirama and Alexander, in their discussions. There was
nothing of the spoilt child about Mirama, but for so small a woman, she
had enough will force for three women. When she put her small foot
down, Alexander Simpson could not make her take it up, although he
weighed almost twice as much as she did. This was very painful to Mr.
Alexander Simpson, who was entirely devoted to Mirama and twice as

sentimental as she, and not half as studious in burning the midnight oil. Indeed, Mr. Alexander Simpson did not possess a literary head, although he thought that he did. Mirama had come out of school at the head of her class. Alexander had come out at the foot of his, and during the year that she had taught under him in the city school she had upheld the discipline and the dignity of the work at the school.

Mr. Alexander Simpson was a fine mathematician and some what of an architect. He had learned the carpenter's trade in his youth, and his father hoped that with a college education, he would become a master carpenter and builder. His father died just before Alexander finished his college course, and as he had a great many irons in the fire at the time of his death, there wasn't much left for Alexander and his mother when all the creditors were satisfied.

Now if Alexander had been a wise young man, he would have taken up his father's business where his father left off. If he had done so he could have saved much of his father's business and property. But Alexander Simpson was not going to bother with the carpentering business, not if Alexander knew himself. He did not think it a proper sort of business for a young man with a college education. Any sort of a common man could be a carpenter, he thought, but any sort of a common man could not be a lawyer.

And just here it was that Mirama Young and Alexander Simpson differed, and so radically that Mirama had put her little foot down and

Mr. Alexander Simpson could not budge it. They had been fighting it over for the hundredth time, this Christmas Eve, and had reached a point where silence had fallen upon them like a wet blanket. Mirama was immovable; Alexander was stubborn.

"I have reached the conclusion that we had better break off our engagement, Mr. Simpson," said Mirama, gloomily, staring into the fire.

"But you can't back out now, Mirama. You have gone too far for that."

"Oh, yes I can!" snapped Mirama. "It is never too late to back out when you find that you have made a mistake."

"But have you made a mistake?"

"Certainly. That is the reason I think it best to break the engagement."

"What is the mistake?" asked Alexander, meekly.

"What is it? Why you are as stubborn as I am, and that I give away to you as much as you do to me."

"Now, Mirama, be reasonable. You know that you are as stubborn as I am, and that I give away to you as much as you do to me."

"That is just it," exclaimed Mirama. "Neither of us ever gives away. One of us must give away. You don't expect me to do it, do you?"

Alexander did not know how to answer this question, so evaded it by asking another: "You don't love me a bit, do you, now?"

"You know I do," [Mirama said] reproachfully; "but you are so stubborn."

"Now, what am I most stubborn in?" asked Alexander, soothingly.

"Everything!" said Mirama, with a sweep of her arm. "Everything! You would provoke a saint." [After a] long pause [she said], "Now, take this law scheme of yours."

"Don't!" said Alexander. "We can't agree on that."

"If we can't agree on that, we shall not be able to agree on anything, and we had better not get married, and I won't marry you. So there!" Mirama had put her little foot down. Alexander argued and coaxed, but he made no headway. He was in despair. Things had never reached this stage before, and a compromise of some sort must be reached.

"What do you want me to do?" asked the strong man, desperately.

"What do I want you to do?" asked Mirama indignantly. "I've told you a hundred times, I want you to give up the idea of reading law, and I want you to stop teaching school, and I want you to go with my father in the carpenter business. You will never succeed in the law, and you don't like school teaching, and you know all about carpentering. My father wants you to help him. He's getting old, and can't attend to all his business. And I am not going to marry you unless you do what I want you to do in this matter."

Alexander had studied the question from a thousand points of view and he had reached the conclusion that the law was the business in life he wanted to follow and that the carpentering business was not up to his idea of dignity. What did he get a college education for; just to be a carpenter? Not much. "You needn't say another word," said Mirama. "I will not budge an inch. The business that was good enough for your father and that is good enough for mine is good enough for you. You couldn't make enough money as a lawyer to support me, and you know it."

"O, I don't think I know anything of the sort," exclaimed Alexander.

"Perhaps you don't," [Mirama said] dryly; "but I do, and I am not going to try the experiment. We don't need to argue the question any more."

Mr. Alexander Simpson did not argue the question any more. He put on his thinking cap and kept it on, in dead silence, for ten minutes. Then a big spasm of pain passed over his face, and Mr. Alexander Simpson, for the first time in their courtship, surrendered.

"I have been trying to get you to fix the marriage day for a year, now, if I do what you want will you fix the date?"

"Certainly," said Mirama. "I will fix the day any time you say after you write your resignation to the school board.

"That is your Christmas test," said Mirama Young.

Alexander took his fountain pen and securing a sheet of paper wrote his resignation to the school board, to take effect at the end of the holidays, and handed it to Mirama. She read it through carefully and said:

"We'll fix the date of the wedding."

"To-morrow, at 3 o'clock," said Alexander.

"O, that is a Christmas test!" exclaimed Mirama.

"Yes; Mirama's Christmas test," said Alexander Simpson.

Three Men and a Woman

Augustus M. Hodges

Augustus M. Hodges

Augustus Hodges uses social criticism to explore key themes in the African-American experience during the 1890s. He takes up such subjects as interracial relations, lynching, miscegenation, racial stereotyping, white liberalism, the "New South," and racism. "Three Men and a Woman" has a didactic tone, as Hodges assumes the role of commentator addressing these topics.

The story hinges around three Christmas Eves, the first in 1890 when the plot is hatched for Ella Watson, a young white woman, to get rid of her husband, Clarence Watson, and to trick her elderly white paramour, Captain Harry Seabergh, into giving her two thousand dollars so that she can be with Jerry Stratton, her black lover. Ella is the granddaughter of Nathan Bedford Forrester, a celebrated Confederate general. The first seven chapters describe how the two schemers accomplish their goal. However, Ella, who later marries Stratton, is not content to just live in New York with him. She longs to visit her relatives in South Carolina. She convinces Stratton, a naive native-born New Yorker, to go to South Carolina with her, where they discover that the "New South" so highly touted in the press is infested with a virulent racism which is intolerant of interracial relationships. On the eve of Christmas 1897, informed by Uncle Tom Tatum of plans to lynch Stratton, they plot their escape back to the North.

The essential question raised by Hodges is what is the significance of Christmas to white southerners? Do they have a "profound reverence and respect for the birthday of Christ," as Stratton believes, or will they "commit murder on a holy day like Christmas or Good Friday"?

In "Three Men and a Woman" Hodges effectively addresses the most salient issues of the time. He explores the myth of black men raping white women and demonstrates that race supersedes any notion of American democratic ideals when the issue is the virtue of white womanhood, that the same forces in control during the antebellum period are in power after the Civil War, and that both miscegenation and violence against southern blacks are widespread.

"Three Men and a Woman" is a fascinating story which falls outside the genre of short stories written and published by black writers of the time. Few black newspaper editors would have published a story such as this. Interestingly, the serialization of the story in the *Indianapolis Freeman* (1902–1903) ended abruptly after the publication of chapter 10, in which the town leaders have decided to lynch

Stratton and Uncle Tom. The newspaper did not explain why the story was being discontinued, and readers were left with a cliff-hanger. It is probable that the story, especially chapter 10, caused quite a stir with Booker T. Washington and his supporters, who would have viewed the depiction of "leading" white citizens as the architects, perpetrators, and manipulators of much of the lynching and violence against southern blacks as highly dangerous. In any case, three months later, in May, the story's conclusion was published without any explanation from the editor. It is likely that the newspaper's readers demanded an ending.

Three Men and a Woman

Chapter I

THE THREE MEN AND THE WOMAN

The time was the year of our Lord 1890, "the night before Christmas"; the place was New York City; the section was No. ———— West Forty-ninth Street, near Fifth Avenue. The place was a "Raine's Law" hotel and ladies' cafe, a place where "respectable" women (white of course) slipped in to have a drink during the day (or night) while their husbands were at work or business; in short, it was a gilded place of vice, "only this and nothing more"—a first class place of its kind.

The hour was 8 at night, while all outside was life and business; inside was dull and deserted. Christmas Eve, almost everybody in Greater New York over 10 years old can be found upon the streets until midnight, either buying Christmas presents or looking at others buy them.

Inside of the "Admiral Cafe," as the back room of the hotel and bar room was called, marched up and down, a colored man, who the layman would call a plain waiter, but who considered himself (and was so registered) as night clerk and steward. He was of a dark brown complexion, little above the medium height, with unmistakable, but "fine" Negro features. His hair, which was of the three quarter blooded Negro grade, was cut short behind and long on top; it was well combed, brushed and oiled, and together with his faultless full dress suit made him look like a statesman, literary man or man of wealth, instead of—what he was.

As he walked the floor from one end to the other, he constantly looked at his gold watch. The echo of his steps resounded upon the marble-tiled "checker board" pattern of the floor. After walking up and down for an hour, he pulled out his watch and remarked to himself: "'Tis quarter to eight and she—"

Just then the street door opened and a pretty young white woman— a blonde—a picture for an artist to paint, entered the cafe—followed by a man below the average in size and mental looks. The colored waiter advanced towards the woman with an extended hand and smile upon his face. She winked her eyes, placed her fore finger across her lips, and remarked in a cold commanding tone: "Waiter, give me a 'bill of fare' until I see what my husband and I will have for supper." (Great stress was placed—with a wise look—upon the words, "My husband"!) The colored attendant put on a sober, business like look and handed the woman a bill of fare. She looked over it a moment, passed it to her husband and without waiting for him to make his selection, said: "Waiter, give us two portions of 'Lobster-a-la-Newbergh' and a bottle of claret." The waiter (as we will hereafter, in this chapter, call the colored man) went to the rear of the cafe, where he yelled the order for the lobster down stairs to the cook. He then went to the bar room where he got the bottle of claret, which he served in the latest style. In a few minutes a colored kitchen attendant brought the lobster and "trimmings" up from the kitchen and turned them over to the waiter, who served the same in great style. He had just done so when the door opened and a stately old man entered. A screen behind the door prevented his seeing in the room.

"Hello Jerry! has that friend of mine—"

The colored waiter raised a warning hand, winked his eye and placed his finger over his lips. The old man took the hint and finished his sentence with: "That friend of mine, Mr. Hopkins, been here to-night?"

"No sir," was the reply.

The old man walked down the cafe and seated himself at a middle row table opposite the woman and her husband. He exchanged looks with the woman, but no one could tell from their looks that they had ever seen each other before. The old man ordered "a small bottle," and made it last until the woman and her husband were gone. A description of the old man is needful: He was a tall, soldierly looking man over six feet, with hair and mustache as white as snow; an ideal picture of the

"Silver King" in that well known play bearing that name, or the mythical "Kentucky Colonel," of whom the funny men of the newspapers write so many jokes about. He was dressed in spotless black, with a long Prince Albert coat and high hat, with a deep widower's band.

The waiter looked at his male guest from head to foot, then went to the mirror and looked at himself. It could be plainly seen that he concluded, that he was the best and most attractive looking of the three men; and he was.

The woman and her husband having finished their supper, she remarked to him: "Wait, my dear, until I find out where the ladies' dressing room is and wash my hands and fix my hair." Turning to the waiter, she asked: "Waiter, where is the ladies' dressing room?"

She was standing with her back toward both men, and she winked her eye and passed a note to the waiter as he was directing her to the dressing room she well knew.

A few minutes after she and her husband left the room, and the colored waiter hastened to read the note. It was printed, or written in capital letters with a pencil, and was in cipher. It read:

"TELL 'NO. 2' TO MEET 'NO. 4' AT PARKER'S RESTAURANT AT 10 O'CLOCK, AS 'NO. 3' GOES TO BRIDGEPORT IN A HOUR. TELL 'NO. 1' TO MEET 'NO. 4' AT 1 O'CLOCK AT THIRTY-THIRD STREET AND SIXTH AVENUE. HAVE A CAB FOR 'NO. 4.'"

Immediately after reading the note, the waiter went over to the old man and said: "Ella says meet her at Parker's at 10 o'clock, Capt."

"Is that her husband?" asked the old man.

"That—is—her—husband," slowly replied the waiter, as he walked away to wait upon other patrons, as the place was beginning to fill up with night patrons. At half past twelve the waiter was "off duty," and after giving instructions to the man who took his place, he quickly put on his street clothes and hurried out to the corner of Thirty-third Street and Sixth Avenue, where he hired a cab; soon after the woman came up to the corner. She and the waiter entered the cab and were driven, by the waiter's direction, to a house in West Sixteenth Street, kept by a colored woman.

The three men and the woman, just spoken of, are the foundation of our story.

Chapter II

THE "WOMAN"

Mrs. Ella Watson, whose maiden name was Forrester, was the grand-daughter of one of the worst "nigger" hating slaveholders and rebels that South Carolina ever produced before the Civil War. She was born in C——, South Carolina, twenty-three years before our opening chapter. Her father was a drummer boy in the Confederate army, and her grandfather a general in the same "lost cause." She had from infancy been taught to hate the Negro and treat him as an inferior, and did so until she reached the age of reason and was a graduate from one of the leading high schools for "F. F. V." young ladies in the mother state of Virginia. The kindness of a male Negro servant, during her last year at the Virginia high school, convinced Ella Forrester that "niggers" were not as black as her people had painted them; that they were human beings like the whites; that they did not make or select their race or color; that their color and birth place (like her own) were the accidents of nature or fate. She at once resolved to treat Negro people as well as she did white people in the same walks of life.

Like all progressive, educated American young women, she did her own thinking, and often wished that the accident of birth had placed her north of the "Mason and Dixon's line," as the granddaughter of a private Union Civil War soldier, instead of the granddaughter of a Confederate general. She visited an uncle residing in Boston and noticed the vast progressive difference between the old North and the "New South," and resolved to make the progressive North her home. Her folks would not agree to this, so she, with a faithful Negro maid, ran away from the God forsaken state of South Carolina to that portion of "God's country" known as New York City, three years before our opening chapter. Her education secured for her a position as book keeper in one of the leading dry goods stores in Greater New York. After she had been with the firm for one year; after she had become a full fledged New York girl; after she had learned its faults and its fashions, its sins and its pleasures; after she had concluded that she would not exist outside of Greater New York, the firm in which she was employed, failed, and she found herself without a penny. She "knew the ropes" by this time, and concluded to get married, as a married woman's certificate (in New York City) covers a multitude of sins, so she took unto herself a husband.

Chapter III

THE "HUSBAND"

Clarence Watson was a native of New York City, a printer by trade—a member of the "big six," and an employee upon one of the leading New York City morning newspapers at the time of our opening. He was one of Greater New York's bread winners, who put all confidence in his wife's honesty in keeping her marriage vows. A year after—twelve months of happy married life—there was a "strike" upon the paper upon which he worked, and the printers' places were filled with non union men, and Watson found himself "on the town" with house rent due. His wife came to his aid, and for several days (and nights)

went to see her relatives (so she said) and each time "borrowed" two or five dollars. They lived on the "borrowed" (nightly) money for several months, when it dawned upon Watson that his wife was not getting the money from her relatives. He had by this time got used to a life of easy living; in which he had his house rent paid, plenty to eat, plenty to drink and money in his pocket to spend.

We all recall the story about the Quaker who told his son: "My son, thee must have money to get along in this world; get it honestly if thou can, but—get it." Clarence Watson soon became a student of this school of philosophy. When he asked his wife for two or five dollars and she handed it to him, he did not ask her where or in what way she got it. In all large cities in the North and West the majority of the men are bread winners—sons of toil—still there is also a large minority who "toil not, neither do they spin," yet they have all the good (and bad) things of life provided by their wives' earnings, and they do not or dare not question the manner in which the money was earned. Watson soon drifted into this class, and when the strike was over and the union printers returned to their cases, he failed to answer the roll call. He informed his fellow workmen that he was living on "Easy Street," and was out of the business. He became a full fledged "sport," "played the races" and "poker" upon the money his wife gave him. When a woman gets a man to this degree, she (womanlike) rules him with an iron hand. When Mrs. Watson wanted him to go out for the night, she

ordered him out, and—he went. When she wanted him to stay in the
house, she ordered him to stay, and he did so.

Chapter IV

THE "OLD MAN"

Capt. Harry Seabergh was, at our opening, a man of sixty-four, a German
by birth, who came to this country with his parents when he was four
years old. His father was a civil engineer and a man of money, who gave
his son a good high school education and then sent him to Yale, where he
graduated with honors. His father died the day the son was twenty-one,
and the mother six months later. Young Seabergh possessed his father's
wealth which he invested in Brooklyn real estate, which paid him about
three hundred per cent. He went to the Civil War a captain in Company
C, 99th N.Y. Volunteer, and was a brave soldier. He married and was the
father of six daughters, five of whom were married at the date of the
opening of this story, and all of them older than "the woman in the case."
His wife, who had been a helpless invalid for three years, died seven
months before the beginning of this romance. He knew she was dying
and went after a doctor, met Ella Watson, flirted with her and took her to
the "Admiral Cafe" and bought her a "wine supper." When he returned
his wife was dead. It has often been said by women in a position to know,

that "an old fool is the worst fool of all," and Captain Seabergh was a living proof that this statement was true to the letter. In the language of the street, Ella Watson "worked him for all he was worth." He gave her hundred dollar bills, bought her diamonds and pearls and fine dresses, and kept the wolf from Mr. and Mrs. Watson's door for many moons.

Chapter V

THE "WAITER"

Jerry Stratton was born in New York City, where his father and mother also first saw the light of day. His mother's maternal parents were Long Island Shinnecock Indians, his father's parents being full blooded Virginians of direct African parentage. He was thirty years old at the time he was introduced to the reader in our opening chapter. He was a graduate of the Brooklyn High School, and had been a law student. He never finished his law course, as the alluring money making position at the "Admiral Hotel" (where he first went for the summer to earn his winter's school money) made him a slave of the "almighty dollar." He was an up-to-date New York City man, no better and no worse than the average man, black or white.

He is the hero, not the angel, of this story, as it has no angels in it. This is not a Sunday school story, although it is a Christmas one. At the time of our writing there were few angels in New York City; human nature and the devil had "cornered the market" in angels.

This romance is written something on the Emile Zola style, to wit: It deals in life as found today in the United States, and shows some of the true relationships of the two races. It is an attempt to prove that the white people of the country (the South especially) are not as pure as they paint themselves, nor the black people as immoral and as bad as the "white folks" paint them.

Chapter VI

KEEPING ENGAGEMENTS

After the woman and her husband left the Admiral Cafe, she hurried him towards the Grand Central depot. He remarked on the way: "Ella, I don't think I'll go to Bridgeport for that job, but try and get one here; I don't want to be so far away from you." The woman looked at him with a firm, commanding look, and replied: "Well, I think you will go there on the next train, or go to the devil. I am not going to house and feed you any longer. You have got to hustle or starve, as my dream of love is over. Here goes your train," and she almost pushed him on the car. She waited until the train left the depot and then hurried down to Parker's Cafe to meet Capt. Seabergh.

He was on time waiting. They entered Parker's, where the old man ordered a private dining room and a "wine supper" at a cost of $25. After the supper and the wine had been served the old man (we started to call him "old fool," but our literary position forbids us from so doing) upon his knees, pleaded to her to leave her husband and go with him. Leave him honorably if she would, (that is, get a divorce) or dishonorably if she must. His seemingly logic was thus: "Now Ella, you are too pretty, too young and too intelligent to spend your time with that beggar you call your husband. He is a man far below your standard, and it is a problem to me how you ever married him. Yes, it is the greatest problem of my life. Now, little girl, listen to me; 'shake' him—get a divorce from him or leave him in any way, honorable or dishonorable, and marry or live with me, and you will never want for this world's goods or pleasures, whether good or bad. What do you say, little girl?"

Ella laughed the laugh of a sharp "woman of the street" who knows her business, and remarked: "Oh, you old sinner! Why is it you old 'lobsters' are always running after young girls almost young enough to be your granddaughters?"

"Love for 'the young and beautiful,' together with the incurable human nature we can't curb, my dear," was the old man's reply.

"I want some money to get a new dress and to spend. Give it to me now and tonight I will, upon my word, seriously think over your suggestion," said Ella.

 Augustus M. Hodges

"How much do you want, little girl," asked the old man, as he pulled out his well filled pocket book.

"Not much, only fifty dollars in small bills," was the reply.

He counted out fifty dollars and handed the same to her. She secreted the money in her stocking, then looked at the clock and remarked: "Well, I must go; I promised my husband to be home at twelve o'clock, and here it is half past the hour; will see you tomorrow night—bye, bye," and she arose.

"But, little girl, you know—"

"No 'buts,' I must go; remember I must spend some time with my husband," she remarked as she kissed the old man and hurried out to meet the colored waiter.

She boarded a Sixth Avenue street car and rode to Thirty-third Street, where she found the colored waiter waiting with an engaged cab. She entered the cab before the driver saw her race and color, and having previously received his instructions, the driver drove to the house in West Sixteenth Street.

The front parlor was lighted when they went up the steps. The waiter rang the bell three times, when the lights at once went out, after which he took out of his pocket a key chain with a bunch of keys and picked out one, opened the front door and entered the dark parlor.

"Is that you Mr. Stratton," asked a voice from the hall.

"Yes mam, Mom," was the reply.

"Well go up to your rooms, they are ready."

With this information they walked up to the parlor and alcove above the ground floor, the best and most expensive rooms in the house. After taking off their coats and hats, Jerry (the waiter) remarked: "There is no place like home."

He rang the bell, and when a servant knocked and the door was opened, he remarked: "Tell Mom to send up a half dozen bottles of Peel's beer, two good cigars, (two for [a] quarter), a broiled chicken, a box of sardines, a bottle of 'Old Crow' whiskey and a package of cigarettes, and have them charged to me."

"Oh, Jerry!" said the woman, "don't have them charged to us, that looks so small for us." Turning to the servant, she said: "Here Sarah, tell 'Mom' to take it all out of this ten dollar bill, and tell her to have a drink on me—I mean Mr. Stratton—and take out a half dollar 'tip' for yourself, Sarah."

Sarah did as she was directed, and soon returned with the several articles and the scant remaining change from the ten dollar bill, when she retired and left the couple "alone in their glory" of disgrace.

After the better half of the food and liquor had been consumed, the colored waiter (who we will hereafter call by his name—Jerry Stratton) lit a cigar, then threw himself on the sofa, while the woman took a seat on a pillow on the floor near his head. She was also smoking—a Turkish cigarette—the kind that nine out of ten young white women of Greater New York smoke.

She smiled as she looked into her companion's face as she remarked: "Say, Jerry, that old 'lobster' wants me to run away with him. Ha! ha! the old fool. He wants me to go out West with him—to California. He says he will give me all the money I want, and—"

"Why, that's dead easy; get a couple of thousands in cold cash from him, go with him as far as Chicago and then shake him, and come back to New York to me."

"I never thought of that, Jerry, I will do it."

"Say, you are dead slow, Ella. If I were a pretty girl like you—well say, I wouldn't do a thing to those old hay seeds."

Before morning the plot was completed. Ella Watson was to get all the cash she could get from the old man, get him to purchase two tickets to Oakland, California, desert him at Chicago and return to New York to her colored lover, which plan was carried out to the letter.

Chapter VII

THE PLOT'S CONSUMMATION

"What story is not full of woman's falsehood?
The sex is all a sea of wide destruction;
We are vent'rous barks, that leave our home
For some sure dangers which their smiles conceal."

—Lee

Ella Watson went as far as Chicago with the old man. During the [trip] from New York to Chicago she blackmailed him into giving her two thousand dollars in small greenbacks. When she got to Chicago she "jumped" the train and returned to New York to her colored lover, Jerry Stratton. The old man was miles west of Chicago before he missed her, as she left him to go to the ladies dressing room to comb her hair (so she said). He did not then realize that he had been "done." The colored Pullman car porter told him that he saw a lady running after the train pulled out of Chicago, and the old man concluded she had left the car and did not return before it started on its California journey. He expected her to follow on the next through train, but she did not. After he had been in Oakland, California two weeks, the truth dawned upon him.

When Ella Watson returned to New York she gave the money to her colored lover, who was diplomatic enough to immediately give it back to her, with the remark: "No, Ella, you keep it; you are the 'banker' of this firm, I am only the 'broker.' You hold the money. I'll do the rest, ha! ha!"

For five years Ella Watson and Jerry Stratton lived together in what they called "bliss." Woman is inconstant; man is changeable. The man of the world who is living an immoral life soon tires of his female toy and gets another one; the woman of the world—woman like—is never true to the man she is supposed to love. She has other toys with which she plays, but—she is careful not to let "a good thing" slip through her fingers. Ella Watson was "only a woman," with all the passions of womanhood of her class, and she rightly guessed that Stratton would soon tire of her, and unless she had some legal hold on him, he would leave her; she therefore resolved to marry him. New York State — God's country — a man or woman can marry the person they want, regardless of "race, color or previous condition." Ella Watson resolved to marry Jerry Stratton. In order to do so she was first obliged to get a divorce from her white husband. In order to do this she took a female companion in confidence — got her to lure Watson to New York City from Bridgeport, Connecticut, to the "Admiral Hotel," where the woman and Watson registered as "Mr. Amos B. Clark and wife." Soon after they had retired, Ella Watson and three witnesses (two of whom were detectives and the third one Jerry Stratton, her lover) broke in Watson's room and got the needful evidence for a divorce — which she got and married her colored lover. She was now Stratton's full fledged wife, with all of a New York State wife's rights. Jerry Stratton borrowed five hundred dollars from his wife the day after they were married and "played the races," winning nine hundred dollars more, all of which he gave her, with the exception of one hundred dollars. With this he played poker and won three hundred dollars more. He then concluded to give up his position at the "Admiral Hotel" and live the life of a sport, but he was afraid his wife (who had all the coin) would treat him as a dependent of charity. The problem of his mind was: "To leave work or not to leave." It was solved for him by the hotel burning down, or more properly speaking burning out, one morning when there was another fire in the same district and the engines were late in getting there. They moved in a "flat" house occupied by white people in One Hundred and Twenty-sixth Street, West.

When they first moved in the flat which was a ground (or first floor one), and the neighbors saw Stratton's dark complexion, they raised an uproar at the idea of living under the same roof with a "nigger," but when Mrs. Stratton told them that she was Spanish and her husband a native of Cuba, who was seldom at home on account of his business, they accepted the situation and tried to be "chummy" neighbors. They did not have the opportunity to carry out their program, as the Strattons were hardly ever home. They rented the flat, which they furnished in great style, simply to have a home, or more properly speaking, an asylum, where they could sleep one or two nights in the week when not elsewhere having "a good time."

Chapter VIII

A VISIT TO THE "NEW SOUTH"

By personal agreement, Mr. and Mrs. Stratton agreed not to recognize each other when it was to their financial interests not to do so. In other words, they agreed that he would not recognize her if he met her on the street with a white person (male or female) that he did not know and she was not to recognize him if she met him on the street with a colored man (she drew the line at a colored woman) and he, fool-like or man-like, accepted the terms. About a year after this agreement, she went to the Grand Music Hall with a white man where, during the play, the song, "The Old Oaken Bucket" was sung, which aroused in her heart a desire to visit the scenes of her childhood.

When she returned home she told her husband—Jerry Stratton of her desire and intentions to visit South Carolina and asked him to go with her.

He accepted. He was not well read upon the social conditions south of the Mason and Dixon Line, [since] he was of northern birth. He did not know that he was going into a lion's den of race prejudice, into a furnace of social fire, into the home of southern Confederacy, into the bed of rebellion, into the mouth of hell, into the devil's country instead of New York, God's country, that he was about to leave. Love or admiration for a woman makes a man blind as to the future, and—Jerry Stratton was blind. They secured Pullman car service to Knoxville, Tennessee, where they transferred to a Jim Crow line to Charleston, South Carolina. He was not aware of the change, as he made the acquaintance of a sporty colored man on the train, who led him into what he concluded was the smoking car, but which was in fact the Jim Crow car. As they were playing poker for money, and Stratton was (by fraud) winning, he did not notice that he was in a Jim Crow car and in ignorant bliss reached Charleston, twenty miles south of C——. During which time he won over three hundred dollars. When they reached Charleston, he and his white wife parted, by a suggestion of his own. He went with his new found friend to a den of vice and she to a fashionable hotel. He won about three hundred dollars at the card table, enough to pay for their visit South. She had a good time in Charleston, as a northern lady. They then prepared to visit C——, the home of her childhood. They hired a "hack," the southern name for a broken down cab, or carriage, which was a hack indeed, [and] drove to C——. His new found friend also went with him to C——. There Stratton and his wife parted, by agreement. Before he left New York City, he purchased several Remington and Winchester rifles, double barrel shotguns and a goodly supply of bird and bear shot and powder, all of which he soon found use for.

After trying to hunt on posted land for three days, during which time he learned the civil, social and political prejudice against his people, he gave it up as a bad job.

During this time his wife had been stopping at the farm of her great uncle's, five miles from the cross-road hamlet of C—— in the township bearing the same name. During her three days' stay at her great uncle's house, she learned the mistake she had made in leaving New York City, God's country, and revisiting C——, the home of her childhood, the devil's land, or she saw her mistake in bringing with her, her Negro husband. Both husband and wife, without consultation or knowledge

Augustus M. Hodges

of each other, resolved to get back home at once—together if they could, separate if they must.

He engaged lodgings under the roof of a two-room log cabin, the home of the Negro who had acted as their guide, or protector, during their hunt on forbidden or posted ground. Jerry Stratton and his wife met, and resolved to return to New York City. "Jerry," she said, "I fear grave trouble for us, or at least you, as the prejudice against interracial social relations are as bitter here as they were one hundred years ago, however, as I led you into this trap I will get you out of it or—we will, more properly speaking, get out of it together. We will stop at your boarding house, at Uncle Tom's for the next few days and then quietly return to New York. Remember my love, [whatever happens,] I will live or die with you."

They passed the next four days in what the romantic author would call "Love's Young Dreams," or what the author of this story calls "blind love." It is a surprising fact to those who do not know the working of the rural districts, how news and gossip can fly so fast in a section of the country where there are no telegraphs or telephones. In three days it was known throughout C—— township, a radius of ten miles, that Nat Forrester's great niece was living with a "nigger" from the North below the village of C——, in the log cabin of old "Uncle Tom Tatum," and of course the righteous (?) indignation of the country folks was aroused to action, and old man Forrester was told to talk to the girl and get her to leave the "nigger" after which the best citizens in the community would lynch the "nigger" and report it as a rape case for the good of the community.

Old Nat Forrester, who was three score and ten and an old Confederate soldier, sent word by a Negro boy to Ella Stratton, his great niece, that he wanted to have an immediate talk with her at his farm home. She, expecting treachery in some form, perhaps kidnapping, refused to go. Old Nat Forrester then rode down to Uncle Tom Tatum's cabin and called her out and remarked:

"Now see here, Ella, you's my brother's gran' darter an' I recon' I'se there only old member of our family. Now, I want ter say ter you gal, that you have disgraced an honorable family of true blue southern people by taken up with a nigger. I don't blame you gal, [cause you] is run away when you was young and I recon' you got mixed up with them d—— Yankees who thinks that niggers are as good as white folks, but they is not. Niggers is only like horses and mules—made to work for white folks. They are not human beings, they have no souls and were only made to be slaves before the war and servants now, they ——."

"Well Uncle Nat, if these people or brutes as you call them are not human, how is it that white men associate with women of this breed? How is it that two-thirds of these people have white blood in their veins? How is it that some 'niggers' as you call them are fairer than some whites? Have not 'niggers' who have white fathers souls? Are not 'niggers' who are as white as ourselves men and women?"

"Well—er—er—well, no; one drop of nigger blood in a person makes him a nigger."

"I can not accept either your terms, logic or your appeal, so good day. You mind your own business and we will attend to ours. We will leave this God forsaken country in a few days, never to return."

With these words she shut the door into old Nat Forrester's face. With a heart full of grief this old gentleman of the "State Rights" state of South Carolina returned homeward. He stopped at the cross road hamlet, known as C—— village where he made his report, the result of which it was decided by five of the best citizens in the community that the girl would be sent to a private insane asylum, and the nigger be burned alive at the stake. So said Jack Nash, the lawyer, and every one said "that's so." It was decided to burn Stratton at the stake after Christmas. Their deep reverence for the Christmas holidays only prevented them taking actions at once.

Chapter IX

FAREWELL PRAYER

"'Twas the night before Christmas," in the year of our Lord, 1897. The time a little after sunset, what they call in the Southland "candle light," that Uncle Tom Tatum rushed in his log cabin, where Jerry and Ella Stratton were stopping.

His face bore an excited and frightened look; his eyes protruded from his head; his nostrils expanded; his lips turned gray; his whole body shook with fear. It was several minutes before he could speak. He at last spoke: "Mister Strattum an' Mist Eller, fo' de Lawd sake; yes fo' hebben sake! please ter go' way; please ter leave my house; please do' git there ole man inter trubble; please don't git me kilt; please—"

"What in thunder's the matter with you Uncle Tom? Are you drunk or crazy?"

"I'se nuther drunk nor crazy, but I wants ter tell yo' all deys comin' to lynch yo' after Christmuss ef dey finds yo' all here, an' dey may lynch me too, so please leave my house ter once. I'se sorry—mighty sorry, but I can't hope it."

"What are you talking about, Uncle Tom?" asked the woman.

"Why Missie yo' see its dis way: de white folks down here don't like ter see yo' messin' wid we black man. Taint right lees more dey don't think it is right. Dey don't like Mistar Strattum an' deys comin ter lynch him, less more, burn him up, less him and yo' gits out of there place ter once, or less more there day after Christmuss; so fer my sake please git out."

During this pleading the old man fell upon his knees, "Ef you don't git out I must; but if I does I'se lose all of my property."

Uncle Tom's "property," outside of the two room log cabin, which was built upon rented land, was an old bed, two broken chairs, an ax,

  Augustus M. Hodges

a hoe, two spades, five plates, two cups, two knives and forks, one pot, one skillet, a sheep's gray homespun Sunday suit and a side of bacon: but they were his, and he did not want to lose them; and had also resolved not to lose his life protecting or harboring a stranger from the North upon whose head was the wrath and righteous (?) indignation of the "best white citizens of the community."

Jerry and Ella looked at each other while Uncle Tom walked up and down the floor in an excited manner. Stratton was the first to speak: "Now see here, Uncle Tom, we can't leave here for three or four days, at least before Christmas, so we will buy you out and pay cash. How much do you want for everything in the place you can not carry away; everything but your personal property? That is to say, to make it plain, what will you take for everything you cannot carry in a bag on your back, and what you can replace new with money?"

"Well," said the old man, after several minutes' reflection, "dey otter be worf $25." Seeing Stratton pull out of his pocket a large roll of bills, the old man added: "Less more dey otter be worf $30 what I leaves hind me. Dey otter—"

"Will you sell me everything in the house, besides what you can carry away on your back, Uncle Tom, for $30?" asked Stratton.

"Yesser," replied Uncle Tom.

"Well, Uncle Tom, here is $100 in small bills, now escape for your life."

The old man stood for a few minutes in mute surprise, before he spoke: "Young man, I'se sorry fer yo, but yo' orter knowed better than ter come down here with a white woman, less more if she is your wife. Yo's got eddykasun; yo' reads de papers; yo' knows how dey—there white folks—down here does our folks. I's an ole man 'bout seventy-five. I can't live much longer, but I does not want ter be lynched. I wants ter live out my time an' go to hebben when I dies. Is yo' got 'ligion or is yo' er sinner man, Mist Strattum?"

"Well, Uncle Tom, I am what you emotional Baptist and Methodist good folks would call a 'sinner man.' I have not got what you would call religion."

"Den I'se goin' ter pray fer yo' soul," replied Uncle Tom. He took off his hat, placed it upon the table, knelt down and motioned them, in a commanding way to kneel; they obeyed. All was silent for two or three minutes. It was silent prayer, (at least on the part of Uncle Tom). At last Uncle Tom began to pray in a low, solemn voice, clear and distinct. He pleaded with the "God of his fathers" not to forsake the American Negro, in this, the darkest hour in his history; he asked the "Supreme Judge" to decide in favor of justice, truth and right. He appealed to the "God of Battles" to fight the Negro's cause for "life, liberty and the pursuit of happiness." He implored the "Prince of Peace" to bring about the friendly relations between the two races that existed before the Civil War, when the interest of "man and master" were one. He imploringly asked the "God of Truth and Love" why it was that the two races

Augustus M. Hodges

could not get along together, as of yore. Was it because the present white folks were better than their forefathers, or were the black people of today worse — more dishonest and immoral than their parents of the days of bondage? He asked the "God of Heaven and Earth" to speed the day when the spirit of prejudice would disappear like the morning mist, as the sun of civilization rises towards its zenith, and men learn, with the aid of a broken education and more enlightened mental vision, that we all have a common heritage of virtues and — failings from whatever race we may be descended. He then prayed for Stratton's salvation, on this the eve of his untimely death, and ended his prayer in the good old Baptist style with: "After all our work is done here on earth, han' us down ter our co'd water graves in peace, and raise our spirrits high and happy in de kingdum is my prayer."

It was an eloquent prayer and sermon. It was delivered in the broken Negro dialect of his section. It was, however, a prayer we hope will be answered in the near future.

They arose and stood in silence for a few moments. Stratton was the first to speak: "Uncle Tom, how in the world am I to be 'handed down to a cold water grave in peace,' if they are going to burn me at the stake? Where did you get that cold water grave business?"

"Why, out of their Bible, yo' knows. Yo' kin read: you' know where to find it in two eye John or some other part; any way I must go, so good bye my son, good bye my gal, God bless yo' both," and Uncle Tom rushed out and was soon lost in the woods.

Chapter X

THE VIGILANT COMMITTEE'S DECISION

Jerry and Ella Stratton watched Uncle Tom disappear in the twilight through the woods; they then faced each other and stood in silence for two or three minutes. Ella at last broke down and burst out in tears: "Oh, Jerry forgive me! Oh, please forgive me for bringing you here to your death; but I will die with you—if they lynch you, they must also lynch your wife. Yes, they must lynch us both. You are the only man I ever truly loved, and a woman will go to and through hell for the man she loves. We will—"

"Keep quiet Ella, until I map out some plan of escape," interrupted Stratton. "I have it; we will take everything we can carry of value and start for Charleston or some other seaport. We will be able to hire one or two horses and wagons and reach the seashore, then we can take the train together (or at least go on the same train) North until we reach Washington. I have learned that even these lawless Negro hating devils have the profound reverence and respect for the birthday of Christ. They would not dare commit murder on a holy day like Christmas or Good Friday; in the meantime as the old saying is: "He who is fore warned is fore armed. I will clean up my rifles and place them and the cartridges upon the table, where they will be handy in case of surprise.

  Augustus M. Hodges

You can't trust these people; I have learned that fact the few days we have been here. I know one thing—"

"Oh Jerry," interrupted Ella.

"Don't interrupt me Ella, you are excited; facts are facts, and the fact of the matter is that we are in a hole and must not stop to debate which one of us got us here, but try to get out. Now there must not be any sleep tonight and at dawn we will start homeward. If we wait until the next day all will be lost, as they will, perhaps, start on their murderous mission the minute after the clock strikes midnight tomorrow and Christmas is a thing of the past until next year. Don't cry, tears will do no good in this case. You cook that wild duck I shot today and make some of Uncle Tom's corn bread, and we will have what may be our last supper together."

Ella started to prepare the supper while Jerry inspected, cleaned and loaded his rifles.

When Uncle Tom was praying for the white folks of the South in general, and those of his section in particular, that God would change their savage, murderous hearts to those of civilized, human and fair-minded creatures, built in the image of God, a scene was being enacted in the cross road hamlet, (the people of the community flattered it by calling it a village). It was a cross road hamlet of about fifty buildings, consisting of three stores, one cotton warehouse, a blacksmith shop, a carpenter shop, two churches and a "tavern" or hotel.

The rest of the buildings were private homes of the "best families" of the county.

Captain Willoughby, the landlord of the tavern, was a little fat old man with a large bald head and sharp dishonest, though business-like eyes. He was what the natives of the community called a "foreigner," coming from New Orleans (so he said) after the close of the War of Rebellion, where he had been the captain of a Mississippi river packet that coined money before the war, bringing slaves from up the river to the New Orleans slave market. The only proof that his statement was true was that he brought with him a bag of gold with which he bought the old "Thompson tavern," which had been closed for ten years, and was slowly rotting down. He patched it up, painted it white, furnished it with second hand furniture from Charleston, thereby filling "a long felt want" in the village.

None but "the best citizens of the community" met there to drink their brandy and sugar or "hot toddy," and perfect their future plans for good or bad. Every lawless act, from the days of the Ku-klux Klans up to the present Christmas Eve, that had been enacted in the neighborhood, was hatched out in old man Willoughby's "setting" room in the tavern. The tavern had a frontage of about sixty feet and ran back about forty feet. The "setting" room was an old fashioned tavern front room of about forty feet square, the floor of which had first been stained with elder berry juice and then oiled with cotton seed oil, giving it a dull "ox blood" red color. In the right hand corner of the room was the bar, over which Captain Willoughby presided. In the middle of the room was a fire place upon which a cheerful wood fire burned on this evening. Around this fire some were seated at the round table near it, and others were standing. Leaning against the mantel piece were seven out of the ten "best citizens of the community." They were according to ages: Dr. Tom Baxter, Lawyer Newton Capps, Mr. John Capers, Mr. Tom Marlon, Dr. James J. Bell, Mr. "Buck" Walker (the richest planters in the section) and Martin W. Sykes, a young theology student, whose father was, and grandfather had been, both ministers of the gospel of the Son of God. The grandfather having had more than a local fame, for his missionary work among the Negroes, whom he taught to fear God and obey their masters, proving (or trying to do so) that they were an inferior race, born and created bondsmen for the whites.

The fortunes (or misfortune) of the Civil War, had left Martin W. Sykes a poor man of South Carolina blue blood, and in order to complete his studies for the ministry, he was obliged to earn every honest (?) penny that came his way. He was the youngest man of the seven, being only 25 years old. He had been at the Baltimore Theological College for two years and had one more year to study before he would graduate as a full fledged minister of the teachings of Christ. Before he went to college he was the local reporter and newsgatherer for the community, and kept the wolf from the door by sending the weekly social and other events of the county to [a] leading newspaper at Charleston. He had also been the Charleston correspondent of the *New York Sensation,* a leading yellow journal of Greater New York City.

Dr. Tom Baxter was the "first citizen of the community." He was 72 and perfectly healthy in body and mind. He had been, in the good old days before the war, the richest slave holder and "nigger trader" in the state. He was at this time a retired physician and extensive planter and the ruler of the county; a hard task master and a hater of "niggers" and Yankees. His word was law. He was a stately old man, wore square rimmed gold spectacles, and a full beard and bushy head of hair—a mixture of deep red and gray.

Newton Capps was about 45 years old. He was the legal light of the county and the owner of one of the three stores. He was the man who fired the balls Dr. Baxter made. Dr. Bell was about 50 and was the leading physician in the section. "Buck" Walker was the leading "truck" planter, who furnished early vegetables and strawberries for the markets of New York, Boston, Philadelphia and Chicago. He always had an eye to business.

Dr. Tom Baxter, Lawyer Newton Capps and the theology student stood with their backs to the fire, while the other members of the "council of war, law and order" were seated around the table discussing the merits of a bottle of brandy and several glasses of hot "toddy." Dr. Baxter advanced to the middle of the group, took his long reed-stem red clay pipe from his mouth and standing erect with a soldierly posting, thus addressed his associates:

"Gentlemen — We do not want to lose sight of the moral necessity of lynching that 'nigger' — burning him at the stake — in the interest of our wives and daughters. This 'nigger' comes here from the North and lives with a white woman — a native of this section, and a member of one of the oldest and most highly respected families of the state. Her grand-father, as most of us know, was a distinguished general in our great war for State Rights. This poor girl (who appears to be demented) ran away North a few years ago and was disowned by an honorable family. Under the teachings of the d —— Yankees, who say that they believe a 'nigger' is as good as a white man, she has disgraced her clan by associating with a 'nigger,' and brings him down here to disgrace us. Why, this is the most bitter disgrace we have ever been subjugated to, with one exception, that was during the war when a company of d —— Yankee soldiers came here, took the place, slept in our beds and forced our wives and daughters to cook breakfast for them the next morning before they marched to Charleston. I say we must burn that 'nigger' at the stake, not later than day after tomorrow, as a warning to our own 'niggers' and a rebuke to the social and civil teachings of these d —— Yankees we all hate in our hearts. Let me say gentlemen, I fully believe, yes know, that all loyal southern white men will hate a Yankee and a 'nigger' for several generations hence."

These logical remarks (from a southern white man's viewpoint) were well taken by those who heard them, and after the majority had expressed their views, which were about the same as their aged leader, it was decided to burn Stratton at the stake the night after Christmas, before the merry makers returned to their distant farms and plantations.

Martin W. Sykes, Esq., asked permission to add a few remarks, and made a timely suggestion. He deplored the action they were about to take; he called the gentleman's attention to the fact that executions or burning at the stake without trial by a jury of white men, (if not a jury of the accused peers), was in the eyes of God and the civilized world, murder; but, he added, that there were exceptions to all rules, and the present case was a grave exception. He deplored the fact that the Negro was so much inferior to the white man; that all the preachings and teachings of the superior race could not raise the poor benighted son of Africa up to the high moral standard for the white brother. He agreed with the other gentlemen that, for the good of the community, it was expedient that they burn Stratton at the stake, but that they hang old man Tom (Uncle Tom) to a neighboring tree for the part he had taken in this disgraceful affair. The only point in which he differed from the rest was that he advocated immediate action that night, and pointed to the fact that delays were dangerous. His point was well taken, and it was decided to lynch the two men that night before 12 o'clock. The several other members of the committee went out to notify the poor whites, who were to do the dirty work, while Mr. Martin W. Sykes remained at the tavern and wrote up for the *New York Morning Sensation* a full account of the lynching.

Chapter XI

THE LYNCHING BEE

Dr. Baxter went to his store, where he informed the poor whites he found assembled there, drinking his corn whiskey, that a "nigger" was to be lynched—burned at the stake—down at the crossroads at midnight. He wanted them all to be there, without fail, and, of course, bring their "shooting irons." He did not tell them what crime the "nigger" had committed, and they dare not ask. To hear Dr. Tom Baxter was to obey him. Then it was of little concern to them whether the "nigger" had failed to lift his hat to Dr. Tom Baxter or had "outraged a thousand of the fair daughters of the Palmetto State."

Newton Capps and Dr. Bell went to the other store and informed the crackers that there would be a lynching that night, just before midnight. They were more considerate than Dr. Baxter, for they told their "poor white" friends that two "niggers" were to be lynched (one burned at the stake) for kidnapping a young white lady and keeping her for weeks in a log cabin, where they had subjected her to all kinds of insults and outrages the human brain could conceive. They were to meet at the old cotton warehouse at 9 o'clock for "instruction," and all promised to be there. The joyful news spread like wildfire. Some ran home to get their guns, others jumped up on the backs of mules and horses and rode out into the interior for ten miles to inform the poor whites that there was to be a "nigger" lynching. Three crackers rode to the neighboring hamlet, London Bridge, seven miles away. About fifty white males averaging in age from twelve to sixty were informed that "the pleasure of their company was earnestly requested" at a "nigger" lynching, and every man and boy (after going home and getting their guns and revolvers) started on a dead run for the hamlet in which the lynching was to take place. Eight o'clock found every white male over twelve years old residing in two counties standing before the old cotton storehouse. The Negro Americans, who numbered ten to one of the white, were conspicuous by their absence.

It had been an open secret for over a week that there was going to be what the whites who had been indirectly informed called fun, and what the Negro Americans called trouble. Neither party knew the exact time the "fun" or trouble would take place, but both blacks and whites had been informed in the usual mysterious way that it would be some time after "Christmas candle light." The wise Negro Americans knew that after "candle light" meant any time after dark, and told the unwise ones so. The result was that every Negro American who was not looking for trouble (and none were) came out to the crossroad stores before noon and exchanged their eggs for "toddy" and whiskey and sugar and went home. The more frightened ones had started for Charleston. The Negro Americans of this section were not cowards, neither were they fools. In the county every male citizen over ten had been restricted from having in his house guns, pistols or other firearms when the local inspector called (after he had informed the whites). In the next county a Negro American could not buy firearms "for love or money." These people knew that "discretion was the better part of valor," and that ten poor whites with repeating guns were brave men when they went out to kill one unarmed "nigger." Facts are facts, and this is simply (from A to Z) a romantic record of facts—a few unwritten pages in the history of "the land of the free and the home of the brave"—God's country, these United States of America. Ten o'clock found every white male over twelve years old, residing within ten square miles of the old cotton warehouse, standing "armed to the teeth" before the warehouse. Dr. Baxter sent down to his store for twenty-five candles and as many potatoes. When he got the same he and Dr. Bell entered the old ghostly warehouse, and while Dr. Bell held one lighted candle the older doctor cut a hole in the potatoes and then cut off the ends so that they would stand upon the window sills of the large gloomy interior of the old warehouse. The number of candles were not sufficient to light up the place properly and gave it a weird light.

The place was soon filled to the door with Negro blood-thirsty white men of all ages and classes, impatient and anxious to receive their last instructions from their leader, Dr. Baxter, before they rushed down the road to perform the pleasant task of lynching a "nigger" or two.

Dr. Baxter stood in the middle of the room upon a dry goods box, and several times stamped his feet and yelled "silence." At last all was still. The pencil of no artist skilled in the drawing of Satan, his imps and their infernal abode could do justice to the scene. Dr. Baxter was short and pointed. He told his followers that a "foreign nigger" had kidnapped a young white woman and had her confined in a log cabin about half a mile below the village at the crossroads. They were going to burn him at the stake, rescue the girl and put her in an asylum (as she had doubtless lost her reason since her forced confinement). The "local nigger," old Uncle Tom, who had been in the past a good, quiet, harmless darkey, was perhaps forced to harbor the "foreign nigger" against his will, or by a big offer of money. In view of his past good record the vigilance committee had decided not to burn him at the stake, but simply hang him as a warning to other weak-minded local darkies. Dr. Baxter concluded by telling them to see that their guns were loaded, but not to shoot unless so instructed by him. There was a lot of old lumber in the corner of the warehouse from which was selected several pieces of chain and rope, after which Dr. Baxter gave the word, "forward march," and the mob, now nearly three hundred strong, made a mad rush down the road towards "Uncle Tom's cabin," where we left Jerry Stratton cleaning and loading his rifles and Ella cooking the supper.

Mr. Martin W. Sykes was at that time just entering Charleston with the forewritten account of the lynching, which he at once telegraphed in full to the *New York Morning Sensation,* which also printed an evening edition, or, more properly speaking, an edition every two or three hours from daybreak to midnight.

It was just half-past 10 that night (New York City time) when the newsboys of New York rushed out of the publication office of the *New York Sensation* with copies of that paper hot from the pressroom. The streets were full of people. One bright businesslike lad, with two perfect lungs, started the cry which his companions took up (several of whom were Negro boys), and soon the air was filled with yells of "Extray! Extre-e-e! Git ther extray. Full account of the lynching and race riot down South. Great excitement in Charleston. Onemanshoterkillsoldierscallout. Oh! get ther extray." It is the custom of New York City newsboys to run four or five words together to excite the curiosity of the passerby and make him buy a paper. The [evening papers] mentioned "sold like hot cakes." Those who bought copies read the following with large full page headlines printed in red ink:

E X T R A ! ! !

RACE RIOT Is Feared IN SOUTH CAROLINA!
Because Two NEGROES WERE LYNCHED
Is Feared That THE STATE TROOPS Will Be
CALLED OUT.

(From Our Special Correspondent.)

Charleston, S.C., Dec. 25.

The beautiful little village of C——, twenty miles south of this city, is in the hands of a mob of wild and excited Negroes, who threaten to murder every white person from the cradle up. As the Negroes in this section number nine to one white person, the citizens have grave fears as to the results. Dr. Thomas Baxter, the leading citizen of the community, has wired the Governor for troops, as more than five hundred armed Negroes are camped just outside of the village.

The cause of this Negro uprising was the justifiable lynching of two Negroes late this afternoon for committing an outrage upon a white girl. The facts in the case are that a strange Negro, claiming to be a Pullman car porter, residing in New York City, came to C—— a few days ago and took up his abode at the log hut of an old Negro, "Uncle Tom," who had heretofore borne a good name in the community with the best white citizen. The northern Negro, Jerry Stratton, spent money freely with the local Negroes at the village stores, hunted on posted land, stared at white ladies, talked impudent to the leading white men of the community, and in several other minor ways made himself obnoxious to the white people. His influence over the local Negroes was soon noticed by their impudence to whites. The climax was reached a few days ago when a young white lady, the granddaughter of a distinguished Confederate general—the hero of the battle of Fort Pillow—was returning home at night fall. She was struck on the back of the head by this northern darkey with a sandbag and dragged for half a mile to the log hut of the old Negro "Uncle Tom," where she was kept for several days beaten, starved and outraged before the facts were known to the white citizens. The old Negro, either from fear or a large bribe of money, failed to report the outrage. The fifth day as he was going to the village store she managed to pin unseen to the back of his coat a note containing the startling facts enclosed in an envelope marked: Help! Read this note! When the old Negro reached the store one of the best citizens in the community saw it, took it off and read its contents. The news spread like wildfire and this afternoon about fifty of the best citizens in the community surrounded the Negro hut, rescued the girl and burned the Negro "Jerry" at the stake. The young lady struck the match herself, and set fire to the light wood which slowly consumed the black wretch. The old Negro confessed all and in view of his past good record was simply hanged to a neighboring tree his body riddled with buckshot and left hanging with a warning to all the local darkies nailed on to his breast on a placard:

Niggers
Take
Warning

The Negroes are arming for revenge and have surrounded the town several hundred strong. It is reported that they have burned several barns and cotton gins and killed three white children a few miles above C——. Great excitement prevails. Dr. Thomas Baxter, mayor of the town, has sent a telegram to the Governor asking for troops to protect the law-abiding white citizens.

Mr. Martin W. Sykes was not sending this dispatch (which he believed was true, in the main, to-wit, that Jerry Stratton had been burned at the stake and Uncle Tom strung up to a tree) "for his health." He kept in communication with the *New York Sensation* until he received a telegraphic money order, and then after some changes and improvements, sold his story to the Charleston agency of the Associated Press in time for it to appear in every morning newspaper of note in the United States on the morning of the 26th. Many of the New York City papers had editorials upon the lynching, and most of these editorials justified the lynching. The few white friends of the Negro, of the good old Charles Sumner stripe, were discouraged and downhearted. The majority of New York City's white population said "it was right," and they would have done the same thing (even in New York) if it had been a female relative of theirs.

We know that more than half of Sykes' story was false. Let us return to South Carolina and see how much of it was true.

Chapter XII

THE ESCAPE

The mob of lynchers rushed down the road towards "Uncle Tom's" cabin. When within a few hundred yards of the cabin, above a bend in the road, with pine woods on either side, the mob gave a yell—the yell all old G.A.R. men who fought on land in the Civil War will recall.

"Silence! D—— you. Silence! Do you want to arouse the niggers and give them an opportunity to escape their just punishment? No more of those yells. March silently until you reach the other side of the bend in the road, then about twenty-five of you go across fields to the right and twenty-five to the left, and surround the house. When the rest of us reach there, knock on the door, and when it is opened pull the niggers out, or if they do not open the door break it in," remarked Dr. Tom Baxter.

The warning came too late. Jerry Stratton heard the rebel yell break out upon the silent midnight air, and remarked to Ella:

"Here they come; put out the lights and do not speak." He was a good marksman, and selected the best of his repeating rifles and calmly cleaned the range glass on the barrel of the gun. "I know these southern gents outnumber me a couple of hundred to one and will kill me in the end, but as I have committed no crime (except coming down here) I am going to sell my life as dearly as I can," remarked Stratton as the mob turned around the curve of the road. The full moon was at its zenith, making the night as bright as day.

The mob, the size of a small army, moved forward, with Newton Capps, "Buck" Walker, Dr. James Bell and Dr. Tom Baxter in the lead. They stopped in the open road, just outside of the range of Jerry

Stratton's repeating rifle. Dr. Tom Baxter pointed the way on each side of the road to the fifty odd men who were to go a roundabout way and surround the house. They advanced. Stratton, with his rifle at his shoulder, sighted them until they were over twenty-five feet within the range of his gun, then he drew a bee line on the first man to the right, Newton Capps, and fired. Bang! Bang! Bang! and three men, Capps, Walker and Dr. Bell, fell to the earth. Dr. Baxter, hearing the shots, and seeing the men fall dead, rightly concluded that the fourth shot would kill him, and he fell a second after the third shot, just before the fourth. The fourth shot struck a man in the next rank in the shoulder, and he dropped down in fear. Stratton had never studied the art or science of war, but it came to him in a minute after the front rank fell, to shoot low and cripple his foes, as it would take two men to take one injured from the field of battle. He fired about twenty-five shots, all but one hitting a mark. These shots caused a retreat—a stampede—of the mob. Some one yelled, "The house is full of niggers all armed. Here they come." The mob rushed backward, their brave leader, Dr. Baxter, in the lead. After they had retreated around the bend in the road, behind the woods, Dr. Tom Baxter regained his courage and thus addressed them: "Boys, that house is full of armed niggers, but we will get them out. Three of you men get into this cart and drive over to my house. In my barn you will find three small cannon we used in the war with the Yankees. I have balls and powder at the store. Bring the can-

  Augustus M. Hodges

non here and we will plant it at the curve and blow the niggers sky high. We will be beyond their range."

Three men started for the cannon, and the rest of the mob went in the old cotton warehouse and waited. When Jerry Stratton saw them retreat, he reached a conclusion. "Hurry up, Ella, and let us pack up and get out, the cowards have gone for more men. They concluded that two hundred (minus those I have killed) were not enough to kill one 'nigger,' and have gone for more brave men," he remarked as he refilled his rifles.

"Hurry up, Ella; pack up all of your things that you can comfortably carry, disguise yourself by putting on a suit of mine, and let us get out. We have no time to lose." Ella did as she was directed without any comment pro or con, a remarkable thing for any woman to do. When they were prepared to leave the cabin Jerry got some flour and rubbed [it] over his face; he then pulled a hunting cap down almost over his eyes and turned his coat collar up. The greater part of his face was hid, and what was exposed looked white from the flour. Ella, with a duck hunting suit, looked like a man instead of a woman, and armed with a rifle each, they prepared to leave the cabin. Jerry took a can of oil and poured it over the floor and sides of the house. He went out in the barn and brought in a keg of turpentine, which he also poured over the floor.

"What are you going to do?" asked Ella.

"Why, set the house on fire, of course. When they see the house burning, they will conclude that some of the braver of their men have stolen up and set the house on fire and burned us up. This will throw them off our track, and prevent them following us."

He raked the hot wood coals out of the fire into the middle of the floor. "Good bye 'Uncle Tom's Cabin,' and good bye (we hope) old Palmetto State," he remarked as he and Ella rushed from the burning house. They stood a few hundred yards down the road to the southward (the same way Uncle Tom had gone). All nature seemed to favor the Strattons in their fight for life. When the attack was made upon them, the full moon made the midnight as bright as day, which aided Jerry to shoot a few of the best citizens of the community. Now, as they took their flight northward, the moon was hidden behind black clouds, and the night was dark. Dressed like two city hunters, they hurried down the road towards Charleston, miles away.

When the house was all of a blaze, Dr. Tom Baxter saw the reflection upon the midnight sky. "The hut's afire. Some of our boys have stolen up and set it afire. Let us hurry down and see the niggers roast," he yelled, as he led the wild mob on a run down the road. When they had turned the bend in the road and were in full view of the burning log cabin, they all stopped. Some one with enough imagination to be a writer of romance yelled, "See them! See them dancing about in the fire? See the girl! Shall we try and save her?"

"No!" yelled Dr. Baxter. "Let her burn with the niggers. Advance and fire at the house, so if any of them get out they will be shot." Immediately about one hundred shots were fired at the burning house. In the meantime the cannon arrived upon the field of battle and was placed in position, loaded and fired several times at the burning log cabin. The fire at last burned out and Dr. Baxter concluded that the "niggers" were all dead, and the party returned to the village. They stumbled over the dead bodies of their brave comrades. Dr. Baxter waved silence. "Pick up those bodies and put them in the cart and take them to the old cotton warehouse," he said to the men nearest to the dead lynchers. They obeyed in silence. "Now, boys," continued the doctor, "we don't want the outside world to know that those niggers killed three white men. We have no telegraph from here to Charleston, and the rest of the world will never know it unless some one here tells it, and the man who does will die like a dog. Remember!"

The outside world has never known until now how three of the best citizens of C—— met an untimely death at the hands of a Negro fighting for his life. Their friends and relatives were told by Dr. Baxter that they were accidentally shot in a deer hunt and so it is recorded.

When Jerry and Ella Stratton had gone about two miles down the road, they met a country cart with two youths about sixteen. They were driving in a hurry, but stopped to ask the huntsmen how far it was to C——, as they were going to a nigger lynching.

"You are too late boys. It is all over. We have just come from there, but if you want to make a dollar each, turn your horse around and drive us in to Charleston or near there. We must be there by daybreak on business of importance. What do you say?"

The boys accepted the terms and drove Jerry and Ella within a half mile of Charleston to the Negro settlement of Lincolnville, where they hired a "hack" and started for the city. During the ride Stratton jumped from the coach and went on foot to the dock of the New York and Charleston Steamship Company, where he engaged steerage passage to New York City. A few hours before the steamer sailed a white lady dressed as a widow secured a first-class stateroom. The good ship sailed. A few days later, as they landed in New York City, Jerry Stratton sang:

> "Home again, home again;
>   Home from a foreign shore;
> Oh, how it fills my heart with joy
>   To be at home once more."

Chapter XIII

THE SEPARATION

The scare Jerry and Ella Stratton got from their visit to the "New South" made an impression on them for about one month, during which time they lived a quiet, respectable life as "Mr. and Mrs. J. W. Brown."

It is hard for "sporting" people to reform in New York City; the temptations are too great, and the Strattons soon drifted back into their fast life. Ella, in fact, tried to make up for lost time. She drank and smoked more. As a result in one year, she looked ten years older. One day, under the influence of liquor, in getting off a car, she fell in the street and was taken to St. Vincent's Hospital in an unconscious state with a cut head. She was out of her mind for two weeks. The account of her falling on the street and being taken to St. Vincent's Hospital appeared in all of the morning papers, and Jerry at once hastened to the hospital to see her. He had forethought enough to say that he had a message from her husband which he wanted to deliver in person. The hospital doctors decided it would not be prudent to show the letter at this time, no matter what the contents might be. They therefore filed it for her reading when she was ready to leave the hospital. Jerry Stratton called every morning for ten days, and when he was refused admittance to the bedside of his sick wife, he went away and wrote her a letter each day. These letters the hospital people filed away and did not give them to her. At last Jerry Stratton concluded that it was a dodge of Ella's to get rid of him, and employed a private white detective to investigate the case. This fellow, who was of southern birth, after hearing Stratton's story in full, took his money, but never went near the hospital. He reported to Stratton that he had investigated the matter, and found out that Ella was not sick, but employed there as a nurse; that she did not care to see him—in fact, she was tired of him, and wanted to get rid of him, and had taken heroic steps to do so. Jerry Stratton believed the detective's lie, and wrote her the following farewell letter:

No. ——— W. 33rd St., New York City.
June 16, 18 ———

"Dear Ella—I have called several times to see you at the hospital. Each time I have been told by a doctor or an attendant that you could not be seen. Each day I wrote a letter [inquiring] about your health and everything, and have received no reply.

"I have positive and well known reasons to know that you are not an inmate of the hospital, but employed there as a trained nurse; that you have (woman like) got tired of your dark-brown top; that you have reflected and have resolved to reform (at least in regards to me). I have in mind an old song, a part of which runs this way

" 'Take her, you are welcome,
But you soon will find it true
That she who can be false to one
Can be the same to two.'

"To which I will fondly and respectfully add that the woman who can be false to two men of her race can hardly be expected—

in fact, can not be expected—to be true to one of the other race. However, Ella, I was foolish enough to conclude, after our down South experience, and the heroic stand you took, that you did love me, and when we again set our feet upon the soil of God's country, we would live together as happily as people in our set, and that you would be as true to me as, well—women of your set. It was all a dream. Yes.

> " 'We are parted from each other,
> And our dream of love is past,
> The bright dream was too beautiful
>   to last.'

"If I do not hear from you in three days, you will never see or hear from me again, and you will be able to conclude without the aid of a doctor, lawyer, judge or jury, my opinion in [the] future of women in general, regardless of their race, color or previous condition.

Jerry Stratton"

About two weeks after this letter was received at the hospital, Ella was pronounced cured of all traces of liquor or cigarette smoking. She had when found a large sum of money, which the hospital people kept for her and returned with the letters of Jerry Stratton a few minutes before she left. She paid all bills due and rewarded the nurses who had attended her. As she started to leave, the letters still in her hand unopened, she remarked to the head physician, Dr. Cross: "Good bye, doctor: I am under lasting obligations to you and all connected with the hospital. You have made a new woman of me physically, mentally, morally and—I am, in fact, almost persuaded to become a Catholic" (the St. Vincent Hospital was a Catholic institution). "Any way," she continued, "I am going to live a purer and better life in the future, and hope when I die that the world will be a small degree better for my having lived in it. Good morning."

She turned to go, when the doctor called her attention to the unopened letters in her hand. After thanking him, she sat down at the table in the reception room and looked at the half score of letters. She at once saw that the handwriting was that of Jerry Stratton. She looked at the postmarks and placed them one by one in a row, according to the dates. She then read them carefully. She then turned to the doctor and said in an angry, excited tone: "Why have you people kept these letters from me so long? I have been in a condition to read newspapers for the past three weeks. Was it because you knew from whom they came? I learn by these letters that several drop letters have been left here for me. Where are they? What right have you to pry into an inmate's private business?" Without waiting for an answer from the surprised doctor, she rushed out and hurried to the nearest telephone station, where she telephoned for a cab and directed the driver to take her to the flat she and Jerry Stratton occupied the day of the accident. Here she learned that he had left there several weeks prior, but left a note with the janitor for her, in which, he said she would find all of their furniture and other goods in the Eagle storage house, rent for the same paid for one year, with agreement for rebate whenever taken out before the end of the year. The note also stated that long before she received it, he would be dead to the New York City sporting world "for the present," and to her "forever and a day" and that he wished her well. The note ended with, in the language of Lord Byron:

> " 'Fare thee well, and—If forever,
> Still, forever, fare thee well.'

Jerry Stratton."

Chapter XIV

HER ATONEMENT

Ella Stratton was a thrice changed woman after she had tried, with the aid of several private detectives, to find Jerry, without success. She knew that he was alive and in some unknown part of the world (or perhaps the United States) laboring under the impression that she had been false to him. She resolved to atone for her past wild acts; she resolved to live a purer and better life; she resolved to do all in her power to better the condition of the poor colored people of Greater New York. Meeting so many old companions who tried to lead her back into the old paths of pleasure and vice, she removed to Brooklyn, where she was unknown, and took board with an old German couple under her maiden name, Ella Forrester. During the day she would walk around in the several sections of Brooklyn where Negro Americans resided and buy food, coal and wood for those she concluded were worthy objects of charity.

One morning she went down town on Fulton Street, in the dry goods district, to make some purchases for herself. As she was about to go up the steps of the elevated railroad station, she felt a heavy hand pull her back. Looking around, her eyes met those of old Captain Seabergh.

"My dear girl, I love you still. Yes, still, although you 'done' me on the train between here and Chicago. You—"

"Unhand me, sir," broke in Ella.

"Oh, I see you are on the stage now. You are an actress. You are, perhaps, the leading lady in some ten-cent play. I will 'unhand' you, as you request me, but I must speak with you, no matter how painful it is to you."

Ella broke away from him and entered the next car. He followed her, but was prudent enough to sit unobserved by her in a corner opposite.

When she left the car, he followed her to her home, or, more properly speaking, her rooms, and entered before she could object.

He threw a check for $10,000 on the table and also placed a roll of $600 in bills on the table. "There, little girl, is your part of my will. I don't believe I will live much longer."

Ella stood up and pointed first to the money and then to the door. "Take back your gold, for [you] will never buy me," she said in a stage whisper.

"Oh!" said the old man, as he took up his check and money, and started to depart, "I will see you again when you are either sober or in hard luck."

Six months later a man called upon Ella at her home; he was Captain Seabergh's lawyer; he informed her that Captain Seabergh was dead — had been run over by a trolley car, that a roll of bills, minus his commission, were hers. The total sum was over nine thousand dollars in cold cash or at least bills (greenbacks and brown backs of small denomination of twenty and fifty dollar bills). The lawyer was gone — the money was there. "I will make this a 'conscience fund' and build a home and mission for needy colored people and name it after my husband, 'Jerry Stratton,'" she said to herself.

In the section of Brooklyn, locally known as "New Brooklyn" is a subsection that, fifty years ago, was owned by Negroes and known as "Weeksville." At the time of the date of our story, there were more colored people in this section than any part of the late "City of Churches." The bad and worthy poor colored people, as well as the good and well-to-do, resided in this section; "Chicago Row," who in "Greater New York" has not heard of the infamous and immoral "Chicago Row"? "Chicago Row" has a history; it was not always "Chicago Row." About twenty-five years before our opening, a German bought a half "block" (or square) of lots, upon which he built a row of houses, which he rented to white people. The house above was also owned by a German, who rented it to a Negro woman of questionable bearings. One by one their places were filled by the lowest Negroes in Greater New York. Chicago Row soon became the home of the lowest Negroes in the section, who were interlarded with poor respectable colored people, who took advantage of the cheap rent. The "Row" spread all over the south side of the block (or square) and then across the street, until the whole block (or square) was composed of Negroes. The vacant lots fell in value. When Ella tried to buy two lots of fifty feet frontage, they were sold to her for a song. She built a mission and home for colored people which she called "The Jerry Stratton Mission and Home for Aged Colored People." In the chapel there was a memorial tablet dedicated to the late Jerry Stratton and a life-size crayon picture of him behind the altar. It was the night before Christmas ten years after the date of our opening chapter. The worthy colored poor had been told to call at the mission that night when they would receive a well-filled basket containing all the parts of a Greater

New York Christmas dinner, and hundreds took advantage of the opportunity. Their donor's heart was made glad, and the "good white lady," as the community called the reformed Ella, received their blessings.

During the winter months each day she gave portions of food and fuel to the worthy colored poor, and as it is often hard to distinguish between the just and the unjust, the good and the bad or the worthy and the unworthy, many a good-for-nothing Chicago Row loafer lived in clover for years. During the week she had kindergartens for the little children, where she taught them to sew and make themselves useful, clean, and neat. At night she had prayer meetings and lectures. She greatly improved the condition of the worthy poor and had some redeeming influence over the lower class of Negroes.

She still remained a mystery to the colored people in general, and the community and city in particular. She was only known as "Miss Ella," and all the children (and some of the aged inmates of the home) declared that she had no other name than that of "Miss Ella."

There were two newspaper men—one black, the other white—who resolved to solve the mystery of "Miss Ella's" past life. To one—the colored man—it was promotion to the staff of his paper; to the other it was cold cash. They searched the records and found out that the property was duly recorded and the trustees of the institution were some of the leading citizens of Brooklyn. The record also stated that the founder was a "Miss Ella Hope."

The colored reporter got the inside track, drew largely upon his imagination (as all Greater New York newspaper men—the author excepted—do) and wrote for the *Brooklyn Eagle* the following:

A NOBLE CHARITY

"The Jerry Stratton Mission and Home for Aged Colored People, situated on Atlantic Avenue, near Troy Avenue, in the section of Brooklyn where the most needy (and candor compels us to say), [and] most depraved colored people resided is a worthy and lasting monument to a noble and benevolent Christian lady, who has the good work under her careful eye, in the person of Miss Ella Hope. The estate has a frontage on Atlantic Avenue of three hundred feet and runs back two hundred feet, upon which are several buildings, the largest being the Old Folks Home, which is five stories high and built in the form of a Greek cross, at a cost of several thousand dollars. Here, all worthy, aged, colored homeless, or poor people can find an asylum the rest of their declining years.

Miss Ella Hope comes from old Abolitionist stock. Her grandfather, General Seth Hope, being one of the Quaker pioneers of Brattleboro, Vermont, where Miss Hope was born fifty-five years ago. Her father was a personal friend of the great Abolitionist, John Brown, and was with him at Harper's Ferry.

When the reporter called yesterday he was shown all over the several buildings by Miss Hope, whose pious face, snow-white locks, kindly, beaming eyes and friendly hand convinced him that this warm-hearted lady was the right person in the right place. At present the institution is in need of a little outside help, and philanthropic people in general and friends of the colored people in particular would do well to send Miss Hope a check so the good work she has started may continue."

Ella did not see the article, and was greatly surprised when she received several goodly checks for the institution.

In looking over his exchanges the Sunday editor of the *New York Recorder* saw the article in the *Eagle* and concluded to write up the institution. He sent a snap-shot man to take pictures of the buildings and a smart young reporter to write it up. After they had taken several pictures of the buildings, the reporter entered, pencil and pad in hand, and commenced to interview Ella. She was surprised and refused to answer his pointed questions. He showed her the article in the *Eagle*, which she read carefully with an amused smile upon her face. When she had finished, she handed him back the clipping without any comment and started for the door; he remained seated, looking about the room writing. This angered her and she remarked:

"My time is of value if yours is not, sir."

"Well, as I told you, I have come to write up the institution and your life."

"I am not looking for newspaper notoriety, and if I were, I would not seek it in the columns of the *New York Recorder*; but —" she concluded, as she took a seat near him — "if you will not interrupt me with questions, I will give a short history of my life and what will in future be my life work.

"I have lived all my life among colored people, I have studied their ways, their good points and their short comings, and have rightly concluded that they are no better or worse than white people. Among them can be found the good and the bad, the just and the unjust, the rich and the poor, the educated and the ignorant, the wise and the simple. The fact that they were born black instead of white was no fault of theirs, but an accident of birth, beyond their control (the same as yours or mine). They did not come here of their own free will, like the whites, but were stolen and taken by force from their sunny African home and brought here as slaves. Since their freedom, all kinds of barriers have been placed in their progressive march to a better civilization by the whites. In the North the stores and trade unions' doors are closed against them; in the South everything, even life, liberty, and the pursuit of happiness, are denied them; still, in the face of all these barriers, the advancement they have made in the past few years has no equal upon the pages of history. Their treatment by a nation claiming to be one of the leading civilized ones of the progressive era is a blot upon the pages of the history of our beloved country.

"The colored people have advanced in every progressive road of life that the white man has trod; they have their eminent divines, their physicians, their lawyers, their teachers, their merchants and their farmers—in fact they have made, according to their small population and average, under untold difficulties, the advancement the whites have made, taking a ratio of the white and black population of the country.

"If they had not been hedged about by a wall of race prejudice, they would have outstripped the whites. My life work is to elevate and improve the condition of the colored people of Brooklyn. Why I have been so moved to do [so] is no business of the *New York Recorder* and I demand it not try to pry into my private matters. This institution is duly incorporated and recorded—the desired information not given by me can be found in the public records at City Hall—good morning," and she politely pointed the reporter the way to the door.

About ten or twelve days after Ella "Hope" (as she is now recorded) gave her Christmas dinner and well filled baskets to the poor of "Chicago Row," the *New York Recorder* published the following upon its editorial page:

A   S T R A N G E   C O I N C I D E N C E

That the world is growing better and brighter; that man's inhumanity to man is growing less as the sun of civilization gets nearer and nearer its zenith, can be seen on all sides without the aid of field glasses; still, the door of charity is often opened by strange hands, as the clipping below from one of our far Western exchanges will show:

[From the Oakland (Cal.) Times]

Three Hundred homeless or poor men and boys of this city were given a Christmas dinner between the hours of 12:30 and 6:00 P.M. at the hotel and restaurant of Mr. Amos B. Clark, on Railroad Avenue, opposite the Grand depot. Mr. Clark is one of our few colored citizens and one of our leading business men and richest property owners. He came here from Chicago several years ago (where, he says, he was born), and with strange foresight bought up all of the then worthless land west of the new Grand depot. He graded the same, built a hotel opposite the depot and built flats upon the rest of his land. These houses are all rented to worthy white people, as there are only twenty colored men residing in the city, all employees in the houses of the rich. The strangest fact about Mr. Clark's dinner was that all of its partakers were white, as there is not a Negro beggar or tramp in the city. Men of Mr. Clark's stripe are a credit to the State, and the Pacific slope, regardless of the hue of their skin, and we hope that Mr. Clark (who, we learn, is a bachelor and worth over $400,000) will continue to be one of our foremost charitable citizens for years, but not as a bachelor, but a benedict.

The strange coincident in the above is that at that time or near about (allowing for the difference between New York and California time) a white lady was doing the same kindly deed for the worthy Negroes of Brooklyn. The coincident points the way to a brighter future, when all Americans, regardless of race, color or other accidents of birth or misfortune will bask alike in the noon-day sun of a "country of the people, by the people, for the people." God speed the day.

The following summer a colored Pullman palace car porter stopped at Amos B. Clark's hotel. He was a stranger; he was talkative. He said he was from New York City and a native of the place. When Clark heard this, he confessed that he was also a native of the great city, and asked many questions about the places and the changes during the past few years. He also asked his guest if he had any New York or Brooklyn newspapers, no matter how old, as news from home was always new news.

The porter told him that he had only a few old papers (mostly Brooklyn ones) wrapped around some packages in his room on the car, across the street, but he would run over and get them. He did so, and gave Clark a bundle of papers about six months' old. As he handed them to Clark he looked into his face and through his full beard, and exclaimed, "As I live! it's Jerry Stratton! Why, Jerry, don't you know me, Ike Randolph? How came you here? How—" The whistle of his train blew and he was obliged to run out before he finished his questions or [heard] the answers to the same.

When he was gone Jerry Stratton (Amos B. Clark was no other) carefully read the papers, which were thick with the history, pictures and the [likeness] of "Ella Hope" and the Jerry Stratton Mission and Old Colored Folks Home. He read them thrice and, as he put them in a pigeon hole in his safe, he remarked to himself, like the stoic he had grown to be, "Her atonement."

SOURCES

Margaret Black
  "A Christmas Party That Prevented a Split in the Church," *Baltimore Afro-American,* December 23, 30, 1916.
Timothy Thomas Fortune
  "Mirama's Christmas Test," *Indianapolis Freeman,* December 19, 1896.
Augustus Michael Hodges
  "The Christmas Reunion Down at Martinsville," *Indianapolis Freeman,* December 29, 1894.
  "Three Men and a Woman," *Indianapolis Freeman,* December 20, 27, 1902; January 3, 10, 17, 31, May 30, June 6, 13, July 4, 11, 1903.
  "The Prodigal Daughter: A Story of Three Christmas Eves," *Indianapolis Freeman,* December 24, 1904.
Pauline Elizabeth Hopkins
  "Bro'r Abr'm Jimson's Wedding: A Christmas Story," *Colored American Magazine,* December 1901.
Fanny Muriel Jackson
  "Christmas Eve Story," *Christian Recorder,* December 23, 1880.
Alice Ruth Moore
  "The Children's Christmas," *Indianapolis Freeman,* December 25, 1897.
Ida Bell Wells
  "Two Christmas Days: A Holiday Story," *A.M.E. Zion Church Quarterly,* January 1894.
Salem Tutt Whitney
  "Elsie's Christmas," *Indianapolis Freeman,* December 28, 1912.
Fannie Barrier Williams
  "After Many Days: A Christmas Story," *Colored American Magazine,* December 1902.